MISCELLANEA

JULIANA HORATIA EWING

Miscellanea

Juliana Horatia Ewing

© 1st World Library, 2007
PO Box 2211
Fairfield, IA 52556
www.1stworldlibrary.com
First Edition

LCCN: 2007930804

Softcover ISBN: 978-1-4218-4847-1
Hardcover ISBN: 978-1-4218-4750-4
eBook ISBN: 978-1-4218-4944-7

Purchase *"Miscellanea"*
as a traditional bound book at:
www.1stWorldLibrary.com/purchase.asp?ISBN=978-1-4218-4847-1

1st World Library Literary Society

Giving Back to the World

"If you want to work on the core problem, it's early school literacy."

- James Barksdale, former CEO of Netscape

"No skill is more crucial to the future of a child, or to a democratic and prosperous society, than literacy."

- Los Angeles Times

"Literacy... means far more than learning how to read and write... The aim is to transmit... knowledge and promote social participation."

- UNESCO

"Literacy is not a luxury, it is a right and a responsibility. If our world is to meet the challenges of the twenty-first century we must harness the energy and creativity of all our citizens."

- President Bill Clinton

"Parents should be encouraged to read to their children, and teachers should be equipped with all available techniques for teaching literacy, so the varying needs and capacities of individual kids can be taken into account."

- Hugh Mackay

PREFACE

The contents of this volume are republished in order to make the Edition a complete collection of Mrs. Ewing's works, rather than because of their intrinsic worth. The fact that she did not republish the papers during her life shows that she did not estimate them very highly herself; but as each one has a special interest connected with it, I feel I am not violating her wishes in bringing the collection before the public.

One of Mrs. Ewing's strongest gifts was her power of mimicry; this made her an actor above the average of amateurs, and also enabled her to imitate any special style of writing that she wished. The first four stories in this volume are instances of this power. *The Mystery of the Bloody Hand* was an attempt to vie with some of the early sensational novels, such as *Lady Audley's Secret* and *The Moonstone*;—tales in which a glimpse of the supernatural is introduced amongst scenes of every-day life.

During my sister's girlhood we had a family MS. Magazine (as our Mother had done in her young days), and two of the stories in Mrs. Gatty's "Aunt Judy's Letters," *The Flatlands Fun Gazette* and *The Black Bag*, were founded on this custom, Mrs. Ewing being the typical "Aunt Judy" of the book. Mrs. Gatty described how the children were called upon each to contribute a tale for *The Black Bag*, and how No. 5 remonstrated by saying—"I've been sitting over the fire this evening trying to think, but what *could* come, with only the coals and the fire-place before one to look at? I dare say neither Hans Andersen nor Grimm nor any of those fellows would have written anything, if they had not gone about into caves and forests and those sort of places, or boated in the North Seas!" Aunt Judy replied that she also had been looking into the fire, and the longer she did so, the more she decided "that Hans Andersen was not beholden to caves or forests or any curious things or people for his story-telling inspirations"; but as it was difficult for the "little ones" to write she enclosed three tales as "jokes, imitations, in fact, of the Andersenian power of spinning gold threads out of old tow-ropes." So far this was Mrs. Gatty's own writing, but the three tales were the work of the real Aunt Judy, Mrs. Ewing herself. These three are (1) *The Smut*, (2) *The Crick*, (3) *The Brothers*. The last sentence in *The Brothers* recalls the last entry in Mrs. Ewing's commonplace book, which is quoted in her Life—"If we still love those we lose, can we altogether lose those we love?"

Cousin Peregrine's Wonder Stories and *Traveller's Tales* were written after Mrs. Ewing's marriage, with the help of her husband; he supplied the facts and descriptions from things which he had seen during his long residence abroad. Colonel Ewing also helped my sister in translating the *Tales of the Khoja* from the Turkish. The illustrations now reproduced were drawn by our brother, Alfred Scott-Gatty.

In *Little Woods* and *May-Day Customs* Mrs. Ewing showed her ready ability to take up any subject of interest that came under her notice—botany, horticulture, archaeology, folk-lore, or whatever it might be. The same readiness was shown in her adaptation of the various versions of the *Mumming Play*, or *The Peace Egg*.

In Memoriam was written under considerable restraint soon after our Mother's death. My sister knew that she did not wish her biography to be written, but still it was impossible to let the originator and editor of *Aunt Judy's Magazine* pass away without some little record being given to the many children who loved her writings. In Ecclesfield Church there is a tablet erected to Mrs. Gatty's memory by one thousand children, who each contributed sixpence.

The Snarling Princess and *The Little Parsnip Man* are adaptations of two fairy tales which appeared in a German magazine; and as both the tales and their illustrations took Mrs. Ewing's fancy, she made a free rendering of them for *Aunt Judy's Magazine*.

A Child's Wishes and *War and the Dead* are more accurate translations, but it may be said they have not suffered in their transmission from one language to another. My sister's selection of the last sketch for translation is noticeable, as giving a foretaste of her keen sympathy with military interests.

CONTENTS

THE MYSTERY OF THE BLOODY HAND

CHAPTER I

A MEMORABLE NEW YEAR'S DAY

Dorothy to Eleanor,

Dearest Eleanor,

You have so often reminded me how rapidly the most startling facts pass from the memory of man, and I have so often thereupon promised to write down a full account of that mysterious affair in which I was providentially called upon to play so prominent a part, that it is with shame I reflect that the warning has been unheeded and the promise unfulfilled. Do not, dear friend, accuse my affection, but my engrossing duties and occupations, for this neglect, and believe that I now take advantage of my first quiet evening for many months to fulfil your wish.

Betty has just brought me a cup of tea, and I have told the girl to be within call; for once a heroine is not always a heroine, dear Nell. I am full of childish terrors, and I assure you it is with no small mental effort that I bring myself to recall the terrible events of the year 1813.

Oddly enough, it was on the first day of this year that I made the acquaintance of Mr. George Manners; and I think I can do no better than begin by giving you an extract from the first page of my journal at that time.

"*Jan. 1, 1813.*—It is mid-day, and very fine, but it was no easy matter to be at service this morning after all good Dr. Penn's injunctions, as last night's dancing, and the long drive home, made me sleepy, and Harriet is still in bed.

"Though I am not so handsome as Harriet, and boast of no conquests, and though the gentlemen do not say the wonderfully pretty things to me that they seem to do to her, I have much enjoyed several balls since my introduction into society. But for ever first and foremost on my list of dances must be Lady Lucy Topham's party on New Year's Eve. Let me say New Year's Day, for the latter part of the evening was the happy one to me. During the first part I danced a little and watched the others much. To sit still is mortifying, and yet I almost think the dancing was the greater penance, since I never had much to say to men of whom I know nothing: the dances seem interminable, and I am ever haunted by a vague feeling that my partner is looking out over my head for some one prettier and more lively, which is not inspiring. I must not forget a little incident, as we came up the stairs into the ball-room. With my customary awkwardness I dropped my fan, and was about to stoop for it, when some one who had been following us darted forward and presented it to me. I curtsied low, he bowed lower; our eyes met for a moment, and then he fell behind. It was by his eyes that I recognized him afterwards in the ball-room, for in the momentary glance on the stairs I had not had time to observe his prominent height and fine features. How strangely one's fancy is sometimes seized upon by a foolish wish! My modest desire last night was to dance with this Mr. George Manners, the handsomest man and best dancer of the room, to be whose partner even Harriet was proud. Though I had not a word for my second-rate partners, I fancied that I could talk to *him*. Oh, foolish heart! how I chid myself for my folly in watching his tall figure thread the dances, in fancying that I had met his eyes many times that evening, and, above all, for the throb of jealous disappointment that came with every dance when he did not do what I never soberly expected he would—ask me. A little before twelve I was sitting out among the turbans, when I saw him standing at some distance, and unmistakably looking at me. A sudden horror seized me that something was wrong—my hair coming down, my dress awry—and I was not comforted by Harriet passing at this moment with—

"'What! sitting out still? You should be more lively, child! Men don't like dancing with dummies.'"

"When her dress had whisked past me I looked up and saw him again, but at that moment he sharply turned his back on me and walked into the card-room. I was sitting still when he came out again with Mr. Topham. The music had just struck up, the couples were gathering; he was going to dance then. I looked down at my bouquet with tears in my eyes, and was trying hard to subdue my folly and to count the petals of a white camellia, when Mr. Topham's voice close by me said—

"'Miss Dorothy Lascelles, may I introduce Mr. Manners to you?' and in two seconds more my hand was in his arm, and he was saying in a voice as commonplace as if the world had not turned upside down—

"'I think it is Sir Roger.'"

"It is a minor satisfaction to me to reflect that, for once in my life, I was right. I did talk to Mr. George Manners. The first thing I said was—

"'I am very much obliged to you for picking up my fan.' To which he replied (if it can be called a reply)—

"'I wish I had known sooner that you were Miss Lascelles' sister.'"

"I said, 'Did you not see her with me on the stairs?' and he answered—

"'I saw no one but you.'"

"Which, as it is the nearest approach to a pretty speech that ever was made to me, I confide solemnly to this my fine new diary, which is to be my dearest friend and confidante this year. Why the music went so fast, and the dance was so short on this particular occasion, I never could fathom; both had just ceased, and we were still chatting, when midnight struck, deep-toned or shrill, from all the clocks in the house; and, in the involuntary impressive pause, we could hear through the open window the muffled echo from the village church. Then Mr. Topham ran in with a huge loving-cup, and, drinking all our good healths, it was passed through the company.

"When the servant brought it to me, Mr. Manners took it from him, and held it for me himself by both handles, saying—

"'It is too heavy for your hands;' and I drank, he quoting in jest from *Hamlet*—

"'Nymph, in thine orisons be all my sins remembered.'"

"Then he said, '*I* shall wish in silence,' and paused a full minute before putting it to his lips. When the servant had taken it away, he heaved so profound a sigh that (we then being very friendly) I said—

"'What is the matter?'"

"'Do you believe in presentiments, Miss Lascelles?' he said."

"'I don't think I ever had a presentiment,' I answered."

"'Don't think me a fool,' he said, 'but I have had the most intense dread of the coming of this year. I have a presentiment (for which there is no reason) that it will bring me a huge, overwhelming misfortune: and yet I have just wished for a blessing of which I am vastly unworthy, but which, if it does come, will probably come this year, and which would make it the brightest one that I have ever seen. Be a prophet, Miss Lascelles, and tell me—which will it be?—the joy or the sorrow?'

"He gazed so intently that I had some difficulty in answering with composure—

"'Perhaps both. We are taught to believe that life is chequered.'

"'See,' he went on. 'This is the beginning of the year. We are standing here safe and happy. Miss Lascelles, where shall we be when the year ends?'

"The question seemed to me faithless in a Christian, and puerile in a brave man: I did not say so; but my face may have expressed it, for he changed the subject suddenly, and could not be induced to return to it. I danced twice with him afterwards; and when we parted I said, emphatically—

"'A happy new year to you, Mr. Manners.'"

"He forced a smile as he answered, 'Amen!'"

"Mrs. Dallas (who kindly chaperoned us) slept all the way home; and Miss Dallas and Harriet chatted about their partners. Once only they appealed to me. What first drew my attention was Mr. Manners' name.

"'Poor Mr. Manners!' Harriet said; 'I am afraid I was very rude to him. He had to console himself with you, eh, Dolly?—on the principle of love me love my dog, I suppose?'

"Am I so conceited that this had never struck me? And yet— but here comes Harriet, and I must put you away, dear diary. I blush at my voluminousness. If every evening is to take up so many pages, my book will be full at Midsummer! But was not this a red-letter day?"

Well may I blush, dear Nell, to re-read this girlish nonsense. And yet it contains not the least strange part of this strange story—poor Mr. Manners' presentiment of evil. After this he called constantly, and we met him often in society; and, blinded by I know not what delusion, Harriet believed him to be devoted to herself, up to the period, as I fancy, when he asked me to be his wife. I was staying with the Tophams at the time. I believe that they had asked me there on purpose, being his friends. Ah, George! what a happy time that was! How, in the sweet days of the sweetest of summers, I laughed at your "presentiment"! How you told me that the joy had come, and, reminding me of my own sermon on the chequered nature of life, asked if the sorrow would yet tread it down. Too soon, my love! too soon!

Nelly! forgive me this outburst. I must write more calmly. It is sad to speak ill of a sister; but surely it was cruel, that she, who had so many lovers, should grudge me my happiness; should pursue George with such unreasonable malice; should rouse the senseless but immovable obstinacy of our poor brother against him. Oh, Eleanor! think of my position! Our father and mother dead; under the care of our only brother, who, as you know, dear Nell, was at one time feared to be a complete idiot, and had, poor boy! only so much sense as to make him sane in the eyes of the law. You know the fatal obstinacy with which he pursued an idea once instilled; the occasional fits of rage that were not less than insanity. Knowing all this, my dear, imagine what I must have suffered when angrily recalled home. I was forbidden to think of Mr. Manners again. In vain I asked for reasons. They had none, and yet a thousand to give me. When I think of the miserable stories that were raked up against him,—the misconstruction of everything he did, or said, or left undone,—my own impotent indignation, and my poor brother's senseless rage, and the insulting way in which I was watched, and taunted, and tortured,—oh, Nelly! it is agony to write. I did the only thing left to me—I gave him up, and prayed for peace. I do not say that I was right: I say that I did the best I could in a state of things that threatened to deprive me of reason.

My submission did not produce an amount of harmony in the house in any way proportionate to the price I paid for it. Harriet was obliged to keep the slanders of my lover constantly in view, to quiet the self-reproach which I think she must sometimes have experienced. As to Edmund, my obedience had somewhat satisfied him, and made way for another subject of interest which was then engrossing his mind.

A man on his estate, renting a farm close to us, who was a Quaker, and very "strict" in his religious profession, had been for a long time grossly cheating him, relying, no doubt, on my poor brother's deficient intellect. But minds that are intellectually and in reason deficient, are often endowed with a large share of cunning and caution, especially in monetary affairs. Edmund guessed, watched, and discovered; but when the proof was in his hands, his proceedings were characteristically peculiar. He did not discharge the man, and have done with it; he retained him in his place, but seemed to take a—let me say—insane delight in exposing him to the religious circle in which he had been a star, and from which he was ignominiously expelled; and in heaping every possible annoyance and disgrace upon him that the circumstances admitted. My dear, I think I should have preferred his wrath upon myself, to being the witness of my brother's miserable exultation over the wretched man, Parker. His chief gratification lay in the thought that, exquisite as were the vexations he heaped upon him, the man was obliged to express gratitude for his master's forbearance as regarded the law.

"He said he should never forget my consideration for him till death! Ha! ha!"

"My only puzzle," I said, "is, what can induce him to stay with you."

And then the storm turned upon me, Eleanor.

You will ask me, my dear, how, meanwhile, had Mr. Manners taken my letter of dismissal. I know now, Nell, and so will not revive the mystery that then added weight to my distress. He wrote me many letters,—but I never saw one!

*   *   *   *   *

And now, dear friend, let me pause and gather courage to relate the terrible events of that sultry, horrible—that accursed June.

CHAPTER II

THE TERRIBLE JUNE

It was about the middle of the month. Harriet was spending some hours with a friend, Edmund was out, and I had been left alone all day for the first time since I came home. I remember everything that happened with the utmost distinctness. I spent the day chiefly in the garden, gathering roses for pot-pourri, being disinclined for any more reasonable occupation, partly by the thundery oppressiveness of the air, partly by a vague, dull feeling of dread that made me restless, and which was yet one of those phases of feeling in which, if life depended on an energetic movement, one must trifle. In this mood, when the foreclouded mind instinctively shrinks from its own great troubles, little things assume an extraordinary distinctness. I trode carefully in the patterns of the terrace pavement, counted the roses on the white bush by the dial (there were twenty-six), and seeing a beetle on the path, moved it to a bank at some distance. There it crept into a hole, and such a wild, weary desire seized on me to creep after it and hide from what was coming, that—I thought it wise to go in.

As I sat in the drawing-room there was a rose still whole in my lap. I had begun to pluck off the petals, when the door-bell rang. Though I heard the voice distinctly when the door was opened, I vow to you, dear Nell, that my chief desire was to get the rose pulled to pieces before I was disturbed. I had flung the last petal into my lap, when the door opened and Mr. Manners came into the room.

He did not speak; he opened his arms, and I ran straight into them, roses and all. The petals rained over us and over the floor. He talked very fast, and I did nothing but cling to him, and endure in silence the weight which his presence could not remove from my mind, while he pleaded passionately for our marriage. He said that it was the extreme of all that was unreasonable, that our lives' happiness should be sacrificed to the insane freak of a hardly responsible mind. He complained bitterly (though I could but confess justly!) of the insulting and intolerable treatment that he had received. He had come, he said, in the first place, to assure himself of my constancy—in the second, for a powerful and final remonstrance with my brother—and, if that failed, to remind me that I should be of age next month; and to convey the entreaty of the Tophams that, as a last resource, I would come to them and be married from their house. I made up my mind, and promised: then I implored him to be careful in his interview with my brother, for my sake—to calm his own natural anger, and to remember Edmund's infirmity. He promised, but I saw that he was slightly piqued by my dwelling so much on Edmund's feelings rather than on his. Ah! Nelly, he had never seen one of the poor boy's rages.

It may have been half-past six when Mr. Manners arrived; it had just struck a quarter to nine when Edmund came in and found us together. He paused for a minute, clicking his tongue in his mouth, in a way he had when excited; and then he turned upon me, and heaped abuse on insult, loading me with accusations and reproaches. George, white with suppressed rage, called incessantly upon me to go; and at last I dared disobey no longer; but as I went I touched his arm and whispered, "Remember! for my sake." His intense "I promise, my darling," comforted me then—and afterwards, Nelly. I went into a little room that opened into the hall and waited.

In about twenty minutes the drawing-room door opened, and they came out. I heard George's voice saying this or something equivalent (afterwards I could not accurately recall the words)—

"Good-night, Mr. Lascelles; I trust our next meeting may be a different one."

The next sentences on both sides I lost. Edmund seems to have refused to shake hands with Mr. Manners. The last words I heard were George's half-laughing—

"Next time, Lascelles, I shall not ask for your hand—I shall take it."

Then the door shut, and Edmund went into his study. An hour later he also went out, and I was left alone once more. I went back into the drawing-room; the rose-leaves were fading on the floor; and on the table lay George Manners' penknife. It was a new one, that he had been showing to me, and had left behind him. I kissed it and put it in my pocket: then I knelt down by the chair, Nell, and wept till I prayed; and then prayed till I wept again; and then I got up and tidied the room, and got some sewing; and, like other women, sat down with my trouble, waiting for the storm to break.

It broke at eleven o'clock that night, when two men carried the dead body of my brother into his own kitchen—foully murdered.

But when I knelt by the poor body, lying awfully still upon the table; when I kissed the face, which in death had curiously regained the appearance of reason as well as beauty; when I saw and knew that life had certainly gone till the Resurrection:—that was not all. The storm had not fully broken till I turned and saw, standing by the fire, George Manners, with his hands and coat dabbled with blood. I did not speak or scream; but a black horror seemed to settle down like mist upon me. Through it came Mr. Manners' voice (I had not looked again at him)—

"Miss Dorothy Lascelles, why do you not ask who did it?"

I gave a sharp cry, and one of the labourers who had helped to bring Edmund in said gravely—

"Eh, Master! the less you say the better. God forgive you this night's work!"

George's hoarse voice spoke again.

"Do you hear him?" and then it faltered a little—"Dorolice, do you think this?"

It was his pet name for me (he was an Italian scholar), and touched me inexpressibly, and a conviction seized upon me that if he had done it, he would not have dared to appeal to my affection. I tried to clear my mind that I might see the truth, and then I looked up at him. Our eyes met, and we looked at each other for a full minute, and I was content. Oh! there are times when the instinctive trust of one's heart is, so far more powerful than any proofs or reasons, that faith seems a higher knowledge. I would have pledged ten thousand lives, if I had had them, on the honesty of those eyes, that had led me like a will-o'-the-wisp in the ball-room half a year ago! The new-year's dance came back on me as I stood there—my ball-dress was in the drawer up-stairs—and now! oh dear! was I going mad?

Juliana Horatia Ewing

CHAPTER III

THE TIME OF TRIAL

Meanwhile he was waiting for my answer. I stepped forward, intending to take his hand, but the stains drove me back again. Where so much depends upon a right—or a mis-understanding, the only way is to speak the fair truth. I did so; by a sort of forced calm holding back the seething of my brain.

"George, I should like to touch you, but—I cannot! I beg you to forgive the selfishness of my grief—my mind is confused—I shall be better soon. God has sent us a great sorrow, in which I know you are as innocent as I am. I am very sorry—I think that is all." And I put my hand to my head, where a sharp pain was beginning to throb. Mr. Manners spoke, emphatically—

"God bless you, Dorolice! You know I promised. Thank you, for ever!"

"If you fancy you have any reason to thank me," I said, "do me this favour. Whatever happens, believe that I believe!"

I could bear no more, so I went out of the kitchen. As I went I heard a murmur of pity run through the room, and I knew that they were pitying—not the dead man, but me; and me—not for my dead brother, but for his murderer. When I got into the passage, the mist that had still been dark before my eyes suddenly became darker, and I remember no more.

When my senses returned, Harriet had come home. From the first she would never hear George's name except to accuse him with frantic bitterness of poor Edmund's death; and as nothing would induce me to credit his guilt, the subject was as much as possible avoided. I cannot dwell on those terrible days. I was very ill for some time, and after I had come down-stairs, one day I found a newspaper containing the following paragraph, which I copy here, as it is the shortest and least painful way of telling you the facts of poor Edmund's death.

"THE MURDER AT CROSSDALE HALL.

"Universal horror has been excited in the neighbourhood by the murder of Edmund Lascelles, Esq., of Crossdale Hall. Mr. Lascelles was last seen alive a little after ten o'clock on Friday night, at which time he left the house alone, and was not seen again living. At the inquest on Saturday, James Crosby, a farm labourer, gave the following evidence:—

"'I had been sent into the village for some medicine for a sick beast, and was returning to the farm by the park a little before eleven, when near the low gate I saw a man standing with his back to me. The moon was shining, and I recognized him at once for Mr. George Manners, of Beckfield. When Mr. Manners saw me he seemed much excited, and called out, "Quick! help! Mr. Lascelles has been murdered." I said, "Good God! who did it?" He said, "I don't know; I found him in the ditch; help me to carry him in." By this time I had come up and saw Mr. Lascelles on the ground, lying on his side. I said, "How do you know he's dead?" He said, "I fear there's very little hope; he has bled so profusely. I am covered with blood." I was examining the body, and as I turned it over I found that the right hand was gone. It had been cut off at the wrist. I said, "Look here! Did you know this?" He spoke very low, and only said, "How horrible!" I said, "Let us look for the hand; it may be in the ditch." He said, "No, no! we are wasting time. Bring him in, and let us send for the doctor." I ran to the ditch, however, but could see nothing but a pool of blood. Coming back, I found on the ground a thick hedge-stake covered with blood. The grass by the ditch was very much stamped and trodden. I said, "There has been a desperate struggle." He said, "Mr. Lascelles was a very strong man." I said, "Yes; as strong as you, Mr. Manners." He said, "Not quite; very nearly though." He said nothing more till we got to the hall; then he said, "Who can break it to his sister?" I said, "They will have to know. It's them that killed him has brought this misery upon them." The low gate is a quarter of a mile, or more, from the hall.'

"Death seems to have been inflicted by two instruments—a wounding and a cutting one. As yet, no other weapon but the stake has been discovered, and a strict search for the missing hand has also proved fruitless. No motive for this wanton outrage suggests itself, except that the unhappy gentleman was in the habit of wearing on his right hand a sapphire ring of great value." (An heirloom; it is on my finger as I write, dear Nell. Oh! my poor boy.) "All curiosity is astir to discover the perpetrator of this horrible deed; and it is with the deepest regret that we are obliged to state that every fresh link in the chain of evidence points with fatal accuracy to one whose position, character, and universal popularity would seem to place him above suspicion. We would not willingly intrude upon the privacy of domestic interests, but the following facts will too soon be matters of public notoriety.

"A younger sister of the deceased appears to have formed a

matrimonial engagement with George Manners, Esq., of Beckfield. It was strongly opposed by Mr. Lascelles, and the objection (which at the time appeared unreasonable) may have been founded on a more intimate knowledge of the suitor's character than was then possessed by others. The match was broken off, and all intercourse was suspended till the night of the murder, when Mr. Manners gained admittance to the hall in the absence of Mr. Lascelles, and was for some hours alone in the young lady's company. They were found together a little before nine o'clock by Mr. Lascelles, and a violent scene ensued, in the course of which the young lady left the apartment. (Miss Lascelles has been ill ever since the unhappy event, and is so still. Her deposition was taken in writing at the hall.) From the young lady's evidence it appears, first, that the passions of both were strongly excited, and she admits having felt sufficient apprehension to induce her to twice warn Mr. Manners to self-control. Secondly, that Mr. Manners avowed himself prepared to defy Mr. Lascelles' authority in the matter of the marriage; and thirdly, the two sentences of their final conversation that she overheard (both Mr. Manners') were what can hardly be interpreted otherwise than as a threat, that 'their next meeting should be a different one,' and that then *'he would not ask for Mr. Lascelles' hand, but take it.'* The diabolical character of determined and premeditated vindictiveness thus given to an otherwise unaccountable outrage upon his victim, goes far to take away the feeling of pity which we should otherwise have felt for the murderer, regarding him as under the maddening influences of disappointed love and temporary passion. Perhaps, however, the most fatally conclusive evidence against Mr. Manners lies in the time that elapsed between his leaving the hall and being found in the park by the murdered body. He left the house at a quarter past nine—he was found by the body of the deceased a little before eleven; so that either it must have taken him more than an hour and a half to walk a quarter of a mile—which is obviously absurd—or he must have been waiting for nearly two hours in the grounds. Why did he not return at once to the house of Mr. Topham? (where it appears that he was staying). For what—or for whom—was he waiting? If he were in the park at the time of the murder, how came it that he heard no cries, gave the unhappy gentleman no assistance, and offers no suggestion or clue to the mystery beyond the obstinate denial of his own guilt, though he confesses to having been in the grounds during the whole time of the deadly struggle, and though he was found alone with scratched hands and blood-stained clothes beside the corpse of his avowed enemy? We leave these questions to the consideration of our readers, as they will be for that of a conscientious and impartial jury, not, we trust, blinded by the wealth and position of the criminal to the hideous nature of the crime.

"The funeral is to take place to-morrow; George Manners is fully committed to take his trial for wilful murder at the ensuing assizes."

The above condemning extract only too well represented the state of public feeling. All Middlesex—nay, all England—was roused to indignation, and poor Edmund's youth and infirmities made the crime appear the more cowardly and detestable.

CHAPTER IV

DRIFTING TO THE END

My misery between the time of the murder and the trial was terrible from many causes: my brother's death; George's position; the knowledge of his sufferings, and my inability to see or soothe them—and, worst of all, the firm conviction of his guilt in every one's mind, and Harriet's ceaseless reproaches. I do not think that I should have lived through it, but for Dr. Penn. That excellent and revered man's kindness will, I trust, ever be remembered by me with due gratitude. He went up to town constantly, at his own expense, and visited my dear George in Newgate, administering all the consolations of his high office and long experience, and being the bearer of our messages to each other. From him also I gleaned all the news of which otherwise I should have been kept in ignorance; how George's many friends were making every possible exertion on his behalf, and how an excellent counsel was retained for him. But far beyond all his great kindness, was to me the simple fact that he shared my belief in George's innocence; for there were times when the universal persuasion of his guilt almost shook, not my faith, but my reason.

There were early prayers in our little church in the morning; too early, Harriet said, for her to attend much, especially of

Juliana Horatia Ewing

late, when Dr. Penn's championship of George Manners had led her to discover more formalism in his piety, and northern broadness in his accent, than before. But these quiet services were my daily comfort in those troublous days; and in the sweet fresh walk home across the park, my more than father and I hatched endless conspiracies on George's behalf between the church porch and the rectory gate. Our chief difficulty, I confess, lay in the question that the world had by this time so terribly answered—who did it? If George were innocent, who was guilty? My poor brother had not been popular, and I do not say that one's mind could not have fixed on a man more likely to commit the crime than George, under not less provocation. But it was an awful deed, Nelly, to lay to any man's charge, even in thought; and no particle of evidence arose to fix the guilt on any one else, or even to suggest an accomplice. As the time wore on, suspense became sickening.

"Sir," I said to him one day, "I am breaking down. I have brought some plants to set in your garden. I wish you would give me something to do for you. Your shirts to make, your stockings to darn. If I were a poor woman I should work down my trouble. As it is—"

"Hush!" said the doctor; you are what God has made you. My dear madam, Janet tells me, what my poor eyes have hardly observed, that my ruffles are more worn than beseems a doctor in divinity. Now for myself—"

"Hush!" said I, mimicking him. "My dear sir, you have taught me to plot and conspire, and this very afternoon I shall hold a secret interview with Mistress Janet. But say something about my trouble. What will happen?—How will it end?—What shall we do?"

"My love," he said, "keep heart. I fully believe in his

innocence. There is heavy evidence against him, but there are also some strong points in his favour; and you must believe that the jury have no object to do anything but justice, or believe anything but the truth, and that they will find accordingly. And God defend the right!"

Eleanor!—they found him Guilty.

*　*　*　*　*

I have asked Dr. Penn to permit me to make an extract from his journal in this place. It is less harrowing to copy than to recall. I omit the pious observations and reflections which grace the original. Comforting as they are to me, it seems a profanity to make them public; besides, it is his wish that I should withhold them, which is sufficient.

From the Diary of the Rev. Arthur Penn, D.D., Rector of Crossdale, Middlesex.

"When he came into the dock he looked (so it seemed to me) altered since I had last seen him; more anxious and worn, that is, but yet composed and dignified. Doubtless I am but a prejudiced witness; but his face to me lacks both the confusion and the effrontery of guilt. He looks like one pressed by a heavy affliction, but enduring it with fortitude. I think his appearance affected and astonished many in the court. Those who were prepared to see a hardened ruffian, or, at best, a cowering criminal, must have been startled by the intellectual and noble style of his beauty, the grace and dignity of his carriage, and the modest simplicity of his behaviour. I am but a doting old man; for I think on no evidence could I convict him in the face of those good eyes of his, to which sorrow has given a wistful look that at times is terrible; as if now and then the agony within showed its face at the windows of the soul. Once only every trace of composure vanished—it was when sweet Mistress Dorothy was called; then he looked simply mad. I wonder—but no! no!—he did not commit this great crime,—not even in a fit of insanity.

"Mr. A—is a very able advocate, and, in his cross-examination of the man Crosby and of Mistress Dorothy, did his best to atone for the cruel law which keeps the prisoner's counsel at such disadvantage. The counsel for the prosecution had pressed hard on my dear lady, especially in reference to those farewell words overheard by her, which seem to give the only (though that, I say, an incredible) clue to what remains the standing mystery of the event—the missing hand. Then Mr. A—rose to cross-examine. He said—

"'During that part of the quarrel when you were present, did the prisoner use any threats or suggestions of personal violence?'

"'No.'"

"'In the fragment of conversation that you overheard at the last, did you at the time understand the prisoner to be conveying taunts or threats?'"

"'No.'"

"'How did you interpret the unaccountable anxiety on the prisoner's part to shake hands with a man by whom he believed himself to be injured, and with whom he was quarrelling!'"

"'Mr. Manners' tone was such as one uses to a spoilt child. I believed that he was determined to avoid a quarrel at any price, in deference to my brother's infirmity and his own promise to me. He was very angry before Edmund came in;

but I believe that afterwards he was shocked and sobered at the obviously irresponsible condition of my poor brother when enraged. He had never seen him so before.'

"'Is it true that Mr. Manners' pocket-knife was in your possession at the time of the murder?'"

"'It is.'"

"'Does your window look upon the "Honeysuckle Walk," where the prisoner says that he spent the time between leaving your house and the finding of the body?'

"'Yes.'"

"'Was the prisoner likely to have any attractive associations connected with it, in reference to yourself?'"

"'We had often been there together before we were engaged. It was a favourite walk of mine.'

"'Do you suppose that any one in this walk could hear cries proceeding from the low gate?'"

"'Certainly not.'"

"The cross-examination of Crosby was as follows:—

"Mr. A.—'Were the prisoner's clothes much disordered, as if he had been struggling?'"

"'No; he looked much as usual; but he was covered with blood.'"

"'So we have heard you say. Do you think that a man, in perfectly clean clothes, could have lifted the body out of the ditch without being covered with blood?'

"'No: perhaps not.'"

"'Was there any means by which so much blood could have been accumulated in the ditch, unless the body had been thrown there?'"

"'I think not. The pool were too big.'"

"'I have two more questions to ask, and I beg the special attention of the jury to the answers. Is the ditch, or is it not, very thickly overgrown with brambles and brushwood?'

"'Yes; there be a many brambles.'"

"'Do you think that any single man could drag a heavy body from the bottom of the ditch on to the bank, without severely scratching his hands?'"

"'No; I don't suppose he could.'"

"'That is all I wish to ask.'"

"Not being permitted to address the jury, it was all that he could do. Then the Recorder summed up. God forgive him the fatal accuracy with which he placed every link in a chain of evidence so condemning that I confess poor George seemed almost to have been taken *in flagrante delicto*. The jury withdrew; and my sweet Mistress Dorothy, who had remained in court against my wish, suddenly dropped like an apple-blossom, and I carried her out in my arms. When I had placed her in safety, I came back, and pressed through the crowd to hear the verdict.

"As I got in, the Recorder's voice fell on my ear, every word like a funeral knell,—'*May the Lord have mercy on your soul!*'

"I think for a few minutes I lost my senses. I have a confused remembrance of swaying hither and thither in a crowd; of execration, and pity, and gaping curiosity; and then I got out, and some one passed me, whose arm I grasped. It was Mr. A—.

"'Tell me,' I said, 'is there no hope? No recommendation to mercy? Nothing?'"

"He dragged me into a room, and, seizing me by the button, exclaimed—

"'We don't want mercy; we want justice! I say, sir, curse the present condition of the law! It *must* be altered, and I shall live to see it. If I might have addressed the jury—there were a dozen points—we should have carried him through. Besides,' he added, in a tone that seemed to apologize for such a secondary consideration, 'I may say to you that I fully believe that he is innocent, and am as sorry on his account as on my own that we have lost the case.'

"And so the day is ended. *Fiat voluntas Domini!*"

* * * * *

Yes, Eleanor! Dr. Penn was right. The day did end—and the next—and the next; and drop by drop the cup of sorrow was drained. And when the draught is done, should we be the better, Nelly, if it had been nectar?

I had neither died nor gone mad when the day came—the last complete day that George was to see on earth. It was Sunday; and, after a sleepless night, I saw the red sun break through the grey morning. I always sleep with my window open; and, as I lay and watched the sunrise, I thought—

"He will see this sunrise, and to-morrow's sunrise; but no other! No, no!—never more!"

But then a stronger thought seemed to rise involuntarily against that one—

"Peace, fool! If this be the sorrow, it is one that must come to all men."

And then, Nelly (it is strange, but it was so), there broke out in the stone pine by my window a chorus of little birds whom the sunbeams had awakened; and they sang so sweet and so loud (like the white bird that sang to the monk Felix), that earthly cares seemed to fade away, and I fell asleep, and slept the first sound, dreamless sleep that had blessed me since our great trouble came.

CHAPTER V

BETWEEN TWO WORLDS

Dr. Penn was with George this day, and was to be with him to the last. His duty was taken by a curate.

I will not attempt to describe my feelings at this terrible time, but merely narrate circumstantially the wonderful events (or illusions, call them which you will) of the evening.

We sat up-stairs in the blue room, and Harriet fell asleep on the sofa.

It was about half-past ten o'clock when she awoke with a scream, and in such terror that I had much difficulty in soothing her. She seemed very unwilling to tell me the cause of her distress; but at last confessed that on the two preceding nights she had had a vivid and alarming dream, on each night the same. Poor Edmund's hand (she recognized it by the sapphire ring) seemed to float in the air before her; and even after she awoke, she still seemed to see it floating towards the door, and then coming back again, till it vanished altogether. She had seen it again now in her sleep. I sat silent, struggling with a feeling of indignation. Why had she not spoken of it before? I do not know how long it might have been before I should have broken the silence, but that my eyes turned to the partially-open window and the dark night that lay beyond. Then I shrieked, louder than she had done—

"Harriet! *There it is!*"

There it was—to my eyes—the detached hand, round which played a pale light—the splendid sapphire gleaming unearthlily, like the flame of a candle that is burning blue. But Harriet could see nothing. She said that I frightened her, and shook her nerves, and took pleasure in doing so; that I was the author of all our trouble, and she wished I would drop the dreadful subject. She would have said much more, but that I startled her by the vehemence of my interruption. I said that the day was past when I would sacrifice my peace or my duty to her whims; and she ventured no remonstrance when I announced that I intended to follow the hand so long as it moved, and discover the meaning of the apparition. I then flew downstairs and out into the garden, where it still gleamed, and commenced a slow movement towards the gate. But my flight had been observed, Nelly, by Robert, our old butler. I had always been his favourite in the family, and since my grief, his humble sympathy had only been second to that of Dr. Penn. I had noticed the anxious watch he had kept over me since the trial, with a sort of sad amusement. I afterwards learnt that all his fears had culminated to a point when he saw me rush wildly from the house that night. He had thought I was going to drown myself. He concealed his fears at the time, however, and only said—

"What be the matter, Miss Dorothy?"

"Is that you, Robert?" I said. "Come here. Look! Do you see?"

"See what?" he said.

"Don't you see anything?" I said. "No light? Nothing?"

"Nothin' whatever," said Robert, decidedly; "it be as dark as pitch."

I stood silent, gazing at the apparition, which, having reached the gate, was slowly re-advancing. If it were fancy, why did it not vanish? I rubbed my eyes, but it was there still. Robert interrupted me, solemnly—

"Miss Dorothy, do *you* see anything?"

"Robert," I said, "you are a faithful friend. Listen! I see before me the lost hand of your dead master. I know it by the sapphire ring. It is surrounded by a pale light, and moves slowly. My sister has seen it three times in her sleep; and I see it now with my waking eyes. You may laugh, Robert; but it is too true."

I was not prepared for the indignant reply:

"Laugh, Miss Dorothy! The Lord forbid! If so be you do see anything, and it should be the Lord's will to reveal anything about poor dear Master Edmund to you as loved him, and is his sister, who am I that I should laugh? My mother had a cousin (many a time has she told me the story) as married a sailor (he was mate on board a vessel bound for the West Indies), and one night, about three weeks after her husband had—"

"Robert!" I said, "you shall tell me that story another day with pleasure; but no time is to be lost now. I mean to follow the hand: will you come with me and take care of me?"

"Go in, ma'am," he said; "wrap up warm, and put on thick shoes, and come quietly down to this door. I'll just slip in and quiet the servants, and meet you."

"And bring a lantern," I said; "this light does not light you."

In five minutes we were there again; and the hand was vivid as ever.

"Do you see it now?" whispered the butler, anxiously.

"Yes," I said; "it is moving."

"Go on," he said; "I will keep close behind you."

It was pitch dark, and, except for the gleaming hand, and the erratic circles of light cast by the lantern, we could see nothing. The hand gradually moved faster, increasing to a good walking pace, passing over the garden-gate and leading us on till I completely lost knowledge of our position; but still we went steadily forward. At last we got into a road, and went along by a wall; and, after a few steps, the hand, which was before me, moved sharply aside.

"Robert," I said, "it has gone over a gate—we must go too! Where are we?"

He answered, in a tone of the deepest horror—

"Miss Dorothy! for the Lord's sake, think what you are doing, and let us turn back while we can! You've had sore affliction; but it's an awful thing to bring an innocent man to trouble."

"The innocent man *is* in trouble!" I said, passionately. "Is it nothing that he should die, if truth could save him? You may go back if you like; but I shall go on. Tell me, whose place is this?"

"Never mind, my dear young lady," he said, soothingly. "Go on, and the Lord be with you! But be careful. You're sure you see it now?"

"Certain," I said. "It is moving. Come on."

We went forward, and I heard a click behind me.

"What is that?" I said.

"Hush!" he whispered; "make no noise! It was my pistol. Go gently, my dear young lady. It is a farmyard, and you may stumble."

"It has stopped over a building!" I whispered.

"Not the house!" he returned, hoarsely.

"I am going on," I said. "Here we are. What is it? Whose is it?"

He came close to me, and whispered solemnly—

"Miss Dorothy! be brave, and make no noise! We are in Farmer Parker's yard; and this is a barn."

Then the terror came over me.

"Let us turn back," I said. "You are right. One may bear one's own troubles, but not drag in other people. Take me home!"

But Robert would not take me home; and my courage came back, and I held the lantern whilst he unfastened the door. Then the ghastly hand passed into the barn, and we followed it.

"It has stopped in the far corner," I said. "There seems to be wood or something."

"It's bundles of wood," he whispered. "I know the place. Sit down, and tell me if it moves."

I sat down, and waited long and wearily, while he moved heavy bundles of firewood, pausing now and then to ask, "Is it here still?" At last he asked no more; and in a quarter of an hour he only spoke once: then it was to say—

"This plank has been moved."

After a while he came away to look for a spade. He found one, and went back again. At last a smothered sound made me spring up and rush to him; but he met me, driving me back.

"I beg of you, dear Miss Dorothy, keep away. Have you a handkerchief with you?"

I had one, and gave it to him. His hands were covered with earth. He had only just gone back again when I gave a cry—

"Robert! *It has gone!*"

He came up to me, keeping one hand behind him.

"Miss Dorothy, if ever you were good and brave, hold out now!"

I beat my hands together—"It has gone! It has gone!"

"It has not gone!" he said. "Master Edmund's hand is in this handkerchief. It has been buried under a plank of the flooring!"

I gasped, "Let me see it!"

But he would not. "No, no! my dear lady, you must not—cannot. I only knew it by the ring!"

Then he made me sit down again, whilst he replaced the firewood; and then, with the utmost quietness, we set out to return, I holding the lantern in one hand, and with the other clinging to his arm (for the apparition that had been my guide before was gone), and he carrying the awful relic in his other hand. Once, as we were leaving the yard, he whispered—

"Look!"

"I see nothing," said I.

"Hold up your lantern," he whispered.

"There is nothing but the dog-kennel," I said.

"Miss Dorothy," he said, "*the dog has not barked tonight!*"

By the time we reached home, my mind had fully realized the importance of our discovery, and the terribly short time left us in which to profit by it, supposing, as I fully believed, that it was the first step to the vindication of George's innocence. As we turned into the gate, Robert, who had been silent for some time broke out—

"Miss Dorothy! Mr. George Manners is as innocent as I am; and God forgive us all for doubting him! What shall we do?"

"I am going up to town," I said, "and you are going with me. We will go to Dr. Penn. He has a lodging close by the prison: I have the address. At eight o'clock to-morrow the king himself could not undo this injustice. We have, let me see, how many hours?"

Robert pulled out his old silver watch and brought it to the lantern.

"It is twenty minutes to twelve."

"Rather more than eight hours. Heaven help us! You will get something to eat, Robert, and put the horses at once into the chariot. I will be ready."

I went straight up-stairs, and met Harriet at the door. I pushed her back into the room and took her hands.

"Harriet! Robert has found poor Edmund's hand, *with the ring*, buried under some wood in Thomas Parker's barn. I am going up to town with him at once, to put the matter into Dr. Penn's hands, and save George Manners' life, if it be not too late."

She wrenched her hands away, and flung herself at my feet. I never saw such a change come over any face. She had had time in the (what must have been) anxious interval of our absence, for some painful enough reflection, and my announcement had broken through the blindness of a selfish mind, and found its way where she seldom let anything come—to her feelings.

"Oh, Dolly! Dolly! will you ever forgive me? Why did I not tell you before? But I thought it was only a dream. And indeed, indeed I thought Mr. Manners had done it. But that man Parker! If it had not been for Mr. Manners being found there, I should have sworn that Parker had done it. Dolly! I saw him that night. He came in and helped. And once I saw him look at Mr. Manners with such a strange expression, and he seemed so anxious to make him say that it was a quarrel, and that he had done it in self-defence. But you know I thought it must be Mr. Manners—and I did so love poor Edmund!"

And she lay sobbing in agony on the ground. I said—

"My love, I pray that it is not too late: but we must not waste time. Help me *now*, Harriet!"

She sprang up at once.

"Yes! you must have food. You shall go. I shall not go with you. I am not worthy, but I will pray till you come back again."

I said, "There is one most important thing for you to do. Let no soul go out or come into the house till I return, or some gossip will bring it to Parker's ears that we have gone to London."

Harriet promised, and rushed off to get me food and wine. With her own hands she filled a hot-water bottle for my feet in the chariot, supplied my purse with gold, and sewed some notes up in my stays; and (as if anxious to crowd into this one occasion all the long-withheld offices of sisterly kindness) came in with her arms full of a beautiful set of sables that belonged to her—cloak, cuffs, muff, etc.—and in these she dressed me. And then we fell into each others arms, and I wept upon her neck the first tears I had shed that day. As I stood on the doorstep, she held up the candle and looked at me.

"My dear!" she said, "how pretty your sweet face does look out of those great furs! You shall keep them always."

Dear Harriet! Her one idea—beauty. I suppose the "ruling passion," whatever it may be, is strong with all of us, even in the face of death. Moreover, hers was one of those shallow minds that seem instinctively to escape by any avenue from a painful subject; and by the time that I was in the chariot, she had got over the first shock, and there was an almost infectious cheerfulness in her farewell.

"It *must* be all right, Dolly!"

Then I fell back, and we started. The warm light of the open door became a speck, and then nothing; and in the long dark drive, when every footfall of the horses seemed to consume an age, the sickening agony of suspense was almost intolerable. Oh, my dear! never, never shall I forget that night. The black trees and hedges whirling past us in the darkness, always the same, like an enchanted drive; then the endless suburbs, and at last the streets where people lounged in corners and stopped the way, as if every second of time were not worth a king's ransom; and sedan-chairs trotted lightly home from gay parties as if life were not one long tragedy. Once the way was stopped, once we lost it. That mistake nearly killed me. At last a watchman helped us to the little by-street where Dr. Penn was lodging, near which a loud sound of carpenters' work and hurrying groups of people puzzled me exceedingly. After much knocking, an upper window was opened and a head put out, and my dear friend's dear voice called to us. I sprang out on to the pavement and cried—

"Dr. Penn, this is Dorothy."

He came down and took us in, and then (my voice failing) Robert explained to him the nature of our errand, and showed him the ghastly proof. Dr. Penn came back to me.

"My love," he said, "you must come up-stairs and rest."

"Rest!" I shrieked, "never! Get your hat, doctor, and come quickly. Let us go to the king. Let us do something. We have very little time, and he must be saved."

I believe I was very unreasonable; I fear that I delayed them some minutes before good Dr. Penn could persuade me that I should only be a hindrance, that he would do everything that was possible, and could do so much better with no one but Robert.

"My love," he said, "trust me. To obey is better than sacrifice!"

I went up-stairs into the dingy little sitting-room, and he went to call his landlady—"a good woman," he said: "I have known her long." Then he went away, and Robert with him, to the house of the Home Secretary.

It was three o'clock. Five hours still!

I sat staring at the sprawling paper on the walls, and at the long snuff of the candle that Dr. Penn had lighted, and at a framed piece of embroidery, representing Abraham sacrificing Isaac, that hung upon the wall. Were there no succouring angels now?

The door opened, and I looked wearily round. A motherly woman, with black eyes, fat cheeks, and a fat wedding-ring, stood curtseying at the door. I said, "I think you are Dr. Penn's landlady? He says you are very good. Pray come in."

Then I dropped my head on my hand again, and stared vacantly as before. Exhaustion had almost become stupor, and it was in a sort of dream that I watched the stout figure moving softly to and fro, lighting the fire, and bringing an air of comfort over the dreary little parlour. Then she was gone for a little bit, and I felt a little more lonely and weary; and then I heard that cheerful clatter, commonly so grateful to feminine exhaustion, and the good woman entered with a toasted glow upon her face, bearing a tray with tea, and such hospitable accompaniments as she could command. She set them down and came up to me with an air of determination.

"My dear, you must be a good young lady and take some tea. We all have our troubles, but a good heart goes a long way."

Her pitying face broke me down. How sadly without feminine sympathy I had been through all my troubles I had never felt as I felt it now that it had come. I fairly dropped my head upon her shoulder and sobbed out the apparently irrelevant remark—

"Dear madam, I have no mother!"

She understood me, and flinging her arms round me sobbed louder than I. It would have been wicked to offer further resistance. She brought down pillows, covered them with a red shawl, and propped me up till the horsehair sofa became an easy couch, and with mixed tears and smiles I contrived to swallow a few mouthfuls, a feat which she exalted to an act of sublime virtue.

"And now, my dear," she said, "you will have some warm water and wash your hands and face and smooth your hair, and go to sleep for a bit."

"I cannot sleep," I said.

But Mrs. Smith was not to be baffled.

"I shall give you something to make you," said she.

And so, when the warm water had done its work, I had to swallow a sleeping-draught and be laid easily upon the sofa. Her last words as she "tucked me up" were, oddly enough—

"The tea's brought back a bit of colour to your cheeks, miss, and I will say you do look pretty in them beautiful sables!"

A very different thought was working in my head as the sleeping-draught tingled through my veins.

"Will the birds sing at sunrise?"

Nelly, I slept twelve long hours without a dream. It was four o'clock in the afternoon of Monday when I awoke, and only then, I believe, from the mesmeric influence of being gazed at. Eleanor! there is only one such pair of eyes in all the world! George Manners was kneeling by my side.

Abraham was still sacrificing his son upon the wall, but my Isaac was restored to me. I sat up and flung myself into his arms. It was long, long before either of us could speak, and, oddly enough, one of the first things he said was (twitching my cloak with the quaint curiosity of a man very ignorant about feminine belongings), "My darling, you seem sadly ill, but yet, Doralice, your sweet face does look so pretty in these great furs."

*   *   *   *   *

My story is ended, Nelly, and my promise fulfilled. The rest you know. How the detective, who left London before four o'clock that morning, found the rusty knife that had been buried with the hand, and apprehended Parker, who confessed his guilt. The wretched man said, that being out on

Juliana Horatia Ewing

the fatal night about some sick cattle, he had met poor Edmund by the low gate; that Edmund had begun, as usual, to taunt him; that the opportunity of revenge was too strong, and he had murdered him. His first idea had been flight, and being unable to drag the ring from Edmund's hand, which was swollen, he had cut it off, and thrown the body into the ditch. On hearing of the finding of the body, and of poor George's position, he determined to brave it out, with what almost fatal success we have seen. He dared not then sell the ring, and so buried it in his barn. Two things respecting his end were singular: First, at the last he sent for Dr. Penn, imploring him to stay with him till he died. That good man, as ever, obeyed the call of duty and kindness, but he was not fated to see the execution of my brother's murderer. The night before, Thomas Parker died in prison; not by his own hand, Nelly. A fit of apoplexy, the result of intense mental excitement, forestalled the vengeance of the law.

Need I tell you, dear friend, who know it so well, that I am happy?

Not, my love, that such tragedies can be forgotten—these deep wounds leave a scar. This one brought my husband's first white hairs, and took away my girlhood for ever. But if the first blush of careless gaiety has gone from life, if we are a little "old before our time," it may be that this state of things has its advantages. Perhaps, having known together such real affliction, we cannot now afford to be disturbed by the petty vexations and worthless misunderstandings that form the troubles of smoother lives. Perhaps, having been all but so awfully parted, we can never afford, in this short life, to be otherwise than of one heart and one soul. Perhaps, my dear, in short, the love that kept faith through shame, and was cemented by fellow-suffering, can hardly do otherwise than flourish to our heart's best content in the sunshine of prosperity with which God has now blessed us.

THE SMUT

The councillor's chimney smoked. It always did smoke when the wind was in the north. A Smut came down and settled on a brass knob of the fender, which the councillor's housekeeper had polished that very morning. The shining surface reflected the Smut, and he seemed to himself to be two.

"How large I am!" said he, with complacency. "I am quite a double Smut. I am bigger than any other. If I were a little harder, I should be a cinder, not to say a coal. Decidedly my present position is too low for so important an individual. Will no one recognize my merit and elevate me?"

But no one did. So the Smut determined to raise himself, and taking advantage of a draught under the door, he rose upwards and alighted on the nose of the councillor, who was reading the newspaper.

"This is a throne, a crimson one," said the Smut, "made on purpose for me. But somehow I do not seem so large as I was."

The truth is that the councillor (though a great man) was, in respect of his nose, but mortal. It was not made of brass; it would not (as the cabinet-makers say) take a polish. It did not reflect the object seated on it.

Juliana Horatia Ewing

"It is unfortunate," said the Smut. "But it is not fit that an individual of my position (almost, as I may say, a coal) should have a throne that does not shine. I must certainly go higher."

But unhappily for the Smut, at this moment the councillor became aware of something on his nose. He put up his hand and rubbed the place. In an instant the poor Smut was destroyed. But it died on the throne, which was some consolation.

Moral.

More chimneys smoke than the councillor's chimney, and there are many Smuts in the world. Let those who have found a brass knob be satisfied.

THE CRICK

It was a Crick in the wall, a very small Crick too. But it is not always the biggest people who have the strongest affections.

When the wind was in the east, it blew the Dust into the Crick, and when it set the other way, the Dust was blown out of it. The Crick was of a warm and passionate temperament, and was devotedly attached to the Dust.

"I love you," he whispered. "I am your husband. I protect, surround, defend, cherish you, and house you, you poor fragile Dust. You are my wife. You fill all the vacant space of my heart. I adore you. I am all heart!"

And if vacant space is heart, this last assertion was quite true.

"Remain with me always," said the Crick.

"Ever with thee," said the Dust, who spoke like a valentine.

But the most loving couples cannot control destiny. The wind went round to the west, and the Crick was emptied in a moment. In the first thrill of agony he stretched himself and became much wider.

Juliana Horatia Ewing

"I am empty," he cried; "I shall never be filled again. This is the greatest misfortune that could possibly have happened."

The Crick was wrong. He was not to remain empty; and a still greater misfortune was in store. The owner of the wall was a careful man, and came round his premises with a trowel of mortar.

"What a crack!" said he; "it must be the frost. A stitch in time saves nine, however." And so saying he slapped a lump of mortar into the Crick with the dexterity of a mason.

In due time the wind went back to the east, and with it came the Dust.

"Cruel Crick!" she wept. "You have taken another wife to your heart!"

And the Crick could not answer, for he had ceased to exist.

This is a tragedy of real life, and cannot fail to excite sympathy.

THE BROTHERS

They were brothers—twin brothers, and the most intense fraternal affection subsisted between them. They were Peas—Sweet-peas, born together in the largest end of the same Pod. When they were little, flat, skinny, green things, they regarded the Pod in which they were born with the same awful dread which the greatest of men have at one time felt for nursery authority. They believed that the Pod ruled the world.

It was impossible to conceive a limit to the power of a thing that could hold so tight. But in due time the Peas became large and round and black, and the Pod got yellow and shrunken, and was thoroughly despised.

"It is time we left the nursery," said the brothers. "Where shall we go to, when we enter the world?" they inquired of the mother plant.

"You will fall on the ground," said she, "in the south border, where we now are. The soil is good, and the situation favourable. You will then lie quiet for the winter, and in the spring you will come up and flower, and bear pods as I have done. That will be your fate. Not eventful perhaps, but prosperous; and it comforts me to think that you are so well provided for."

Juliana Horatia Ewing

But the best of parents cannot foresee everything in the future career of their children, and the mother plant was wrong.

The Peas burst from the Pod, it is true; but they fell, not into the south border, but into the hand of the seedsman to whom the garden belonged.

"This is an adventure," said the brothers.

They were put with a lot of other Sweet-peas, and a brown paper bag was ready to receive them.

"Any way we are together," said they.

But at that moment one of the brothers rolled from the bag on the floor. The seedsman picked him up, and he found himself tossed into a bag of peas.

"It is all right," said he; "I shall find my brother in time."

But though he rolled about as much as he could, he could not find him; for the truth is, that he had been put by mistake into a paper of eating peas; but he did not know this.

"Patience!" cried he; "we shall be sown shortly, and when we come up we shall find each other, if not before."

The other Pea thought that his brother was in the bag with him, and when he could not find him he consoled himself in the same manner.

"When we come up we shall find each other, if not before."

They were both sold in company with others, and they were both sown. No. 1 was sown in a cosy little garden near a cosy little cottage in the country. No. 2 was sown in a field, being intended for the market.

They both came up and made leaves, and budded and blossomed, and the first thing each did when he opened his petals was to look round for his brother.

No. 1 found himself among other Sweet-peas, but his brother was not there; and soon a beautiful girl, who came into a garden to gather a nosegay, plucked him from his stalk.

No. 2 found himself also among Peas—a field full—but they were all white ones, and had no scent whatever. He had been sown near the wall, and he leant against it and wept.

Just then a young sailor came whistling down the road. He was sunburnt but handsome, and he was picking flowers from the roadside. When he saw the Sweet-pea he shouted.

"That's the best of the bunch," said he, and put it with the others. Then he went whistling down the road into the village, past the old grey church, and up to a cosy little cottage in a cosy little garden. He opened the door and went into a room where a beautiful girl was arranging some flowers that lay on the table. When she saw him they gave a cry and embraced each other. After a while he said, "I have brought you some wild flowers; but this is the best," and he held up the Sweet-pea.

"This is not a wild flower," said she; "it is a garden flower, and must have been sown by accident. It shall be put with the other garden flowers."

And she laid the Sweet-pea among the rest on the table, and so the brothers met at last.

The young couple sat hand in hand in the sunshine, and talked of the past.

"Time seemed to go slowly while we were parted," said the young man; "and now, to look back upon, all our misery seems but a dream."

"That is just what *we* feel," said the Sweet-peas.

"I was very sad," said the young girl softly, "very sad indeed; for, I thought you might be dead, or have married some one else, and that we might never meet again. But in spite of everything I couldn't quite despair. It seemed impossible that those who really loved each other should be separated for ever."

Meanwhile the Sweet-peas lay on the table. They were very happy, but just a little anxious, for the lovers had forgotten to put them in water, and they were fading fast.

"We are very happy," they murmured, "very happy. This moment alone is worth all that we have endured. It is true we are fading before we have ever fully bloomed, and after this we do not know what will happen to us. But the young girl is right. One cannot quite despair. It seems impossible that those who really love each other should be separated for ever."

COUSIN PEREGRINE'S WONDER STORIES

THE CHINESE JUGGLERS, AND THE ENGLISHMAN'S HANDS

(*Founded on Fact.*)

Cousin Peregrine had never been away quite so long before. He had been in the East, and the latter part of his absence from home had been spent not only in a foreign country, but in parts of it where Englishmen had seldom been before, and amid the miserable scenes of war.

However, he was at home at last, very much to the satisfaction of his young cousins, and also to his own. They had been assured by him, in a highly illustrated letter, that his arms were safe and sound in his coat-sleeves, that he had no wooden legs, and that they might feel him all over for wounds as hard as they liked. Only Maggie, the eldest, could even fancy she remembered Cousin Peregrine, but they all seemed to know him by his letters, even before he arrived. At last he came.

Cousin Peregrine was dressed like other people, much to the disappointment of his young relatives, who when they burst (with more or less attention to etiquette) into the dining-room with the dessert, were in full expectation of seeing him in his

Juliana Horatia Ewing

uniform, or at least with his latest medal pinned to his dress-coat.

Perhaps it was because Cousin Peregrine was so very seldom troubled by chubby English children with a claim on his good nature that he was particularly indulgent to his young cousins. However this may be, they soon stood in no awe of him, and a chorus cried around him—

"Where's your new medal, Cousin? What's it about? What's on it?"

"Taku Forts," said Cousin Peregrine, smiling grimly.

"What's Tar—Koo?" inquired the young people.

"Taku is the name of a place in China, and you know I've just come from China," said Cousin Peregrine.

On which six voices cried—

"Did you drink nothing but tea?"

"Did you buy lots of old China dragons?"

"Did you see any ladies with half their feet cut off?"

"Did you live in a house with bells hanging from the roof?"

"Are the Chinese like the people on Mamma's fan?"

"Did you wear a pigtail?"

Cousin Peregrine's hair was so very short that the last question raised a roar of laughter, after which the chorus spoke with one voice—

"Do tell us all about China!"

At which he put on a serio-comic countenance, and answered with much gravity—

"Oh, certainly, with all my heart. It will be rather a long story, but never mind. By the way, I am afraid I can hardly begin much before the birth of Confucius, but as that happened in or about the year 550 B.C., you will still have to hear about two thousand four hundred years of its history or so, which will keep us going for a few months".

"Confucius—whose real name was Kwang-Foo-Tsz (and if you can pronounce that last word properly you can do more than many eminent Chinese scholars can)—was born in the province of Kan Tang—.

"Oh, not about Confuse-us!" pleaded a little maid on Cousin Peregrine's knee. "Tell us what you did."

"But tell us *wonderful* things," stipulated a young gentleman, fresh from *The Boy Hunters* and kindred works.

If young bachelors have a weak point when they are kind to children, it is that they are apt to puzzle them with paradoxes. Even Cousin Peregrine did "sometimes tease," so his cousins said.

On this occasion he began a long rambling speech, in which he pretended not to know what things are and what are not *wonderful*. The *Boy Hunters* young gentleman fell headlong into the quagmire of definitions, but the oldest sister, who had her own ideas about things, said firmly—

"Wonderful things are things which surprise you very much, and which you never saw before, and which you don't understand. Like as if you saw a lot of giants coming out of a hole in the road. At least that's what *we* mean by wonderful."

"Upon my word, Maggie," said Cousin Peregrine, "your definition is most admirable. I cannot say that I have met with giants in China, even in the north, where the men are taller than in the south. But I can tell you of something I saw in China which surprised me very much, which I had never seen before, and which, I give you my word, I don't understand to this hour, but which I have no doubt was not in the least wonderful to the poor half-naked Chinaman who did it in my courtyard. And then, if you like, I will tell you something else which surprised some Chinese country-folk very much, which they never saw before, and which they certainly did not understand when they did see it. Will that do?"

"Oh yes, yes! Thank you, yes!" cried the chorus, and Maggie said—

"First all about the thing *you* thought wonderful, you know."

"Well, the thing I thought wonderful was a conjuring trick done by a Chinese juggler."

"Did he only do one trick?" said the little maid on Cousin Peregrine's knee.

"Oh, he did lots of tricks," said Cousin Peregrine, "many of them common Eastern ones, which are now familiar in England, but which he certainly performed in a wonderful way: because, you see, he had not the advantage of doing his tricks on a stage fitted up by himself, he did them in the street, or in my courtyard, with very little apparatus, and naked to the waist. For instance, the common trick of bringing a glass bowl full of water and fish out of a seemingly empty shawl is not so marvellous if the conjurer has a well-draped table near him from behind which he can get such things, or even good wide sleeves to hide them in. But my poor conjurer was almost naked, and the bit of carpet, about the size of this hearthrug, which he carried with him, did not seem capable of holding glass bowls of water, most certainly. Besides which he shook it, and spread it on the ground close by me, after which he threw himself down and rolled on it. And yet from underneath this he drew out a glass bowl of water with gold-fish swimming in it. But that trick and many others one can see very well done in London now, though not so utterly without apparatus. The trick which he did so particularly well, and which puzzled me so much, I have never seen in Europe. This is the one I am going to describe to you."

"Describe the conjurer a bit more first, Cousin Peregrine."

"There is nothing more to describe. He was not at all a grand conjurer, he was only a poor common juggler, exhibiting his tricks in the public streets many times in the day for the few small coins which the bystanders chose to give him. He was a very merry fellow, and all the time he was about his performance he kept making fun and jokes; and these amused the audience so much that you may believe that I was sorry my ignorance of his language hindered me from understanding them.

"All sorts of people used to stop and look at the juggler: brawny porters, with loads of merchandise, or boxes of tea, or bars of silver, which they carried in boxes or baskets slung on bamboo poles over their shoulders."

"Like the pictures on the tea-boxes," whispered little Bessy.

"There's a figure of it in the grocer's window," said her brother, who had seen more of the world than Bessy; "not a picture, a figure dressed in silk; and they're square boxes, not baskets, that he's got—wooden panniers I call them."

"Who else used to stop, Cousin Peregrine?" asked Maggie.

"Street confectioners, Maggie, with small movable sweet-meat stalls, which they carry on their backs. Men with portable stoves too, who always have a cup of tea ready for you for a small coin worth about the twentieth part of a penny. Tiny-footed women toddling awkwardly along, with children—also cramp-footed—toddling awkwardly after them, dressed in all the colours of the rainbow, and with their poor little arms stuck out at right angles with their bodies, to help them to keep their balance. Even the blind beggars, who go along striking on a bell to let people know that they are blind, as otherwise they might be knocked over, even they used to stop and listen to my juggler's jokes, though they could not see his tricks.

"All this was in the street; but sometimes I got him to come into my own courtyard to do his tricks there, that I might watch him more carefully. But watch as I might, I could never see how he did this particular feat. He used to do it with no clothes on except a pair of short trousers, for in the hot season, you must know, the lower classes of Chinese go about naked to the waist. Indeed, hot as it is, they don't wear hats. The juggler possessed both a hat and a jacket, as it happened, but he took them off when he did his trick."

"And what *was* the trick?" asked several impatient voices. "What did he do?"

"He used to swallow ten or twelve needles one after the other, and 'wash them down' with a ball of thread, which he swallowed next, and by and by he used to draw the thread slowly out of his mouth, yard after yard, and it had all the needles threaded on it."

"Oh, Cousin Peregrine!"

"He used to come quite close to me, Maggie, as close as I am to you now, and take each needle—one after the other—between the finger and thumb of his right hand—keeping all the other fingers away from it, stick the point of it for a moment into his other palm, to show that it was sharp, and then to all appearance swallow it bodily before your eyes. In this way he seemed to swallow successively all the twelve needles. Then he opened his mouth, that you might ascertain that they were not there, and you certainly could not see them. He next swallowed a little ball of thread, not much bigger than a pea. This being done, he seemed to be very uneasy (as well he might be!), and he made fearful faces and violent gestures, and stamped on the ground, and muttered incantations, and threw up his hands and eyes to the sky; and presently the end of a thread was to be seen coming out between his teeth, upon which he took hold of this end, and carefully drew out the thread with all the needles threaded on it. Then there was always much applause, and the small coins used to be put pretty liberally into the hat which he handed round to receive them."

"Was that all?" asked the young gentleman of the adventure books.

"All what, Fred?"

"All that you thought wonderful."

"Yes," said Cousin Peregrine. "Don't you think it curious?"

"Oh, very, Cousin, and I like it very much indeed, only if that's all *you* thought wonderful, now I want you to tell us what *you* did that *the Chinese* thought wonderful."

"It's not very easy to surprise a town-bred Chinaman," said Cousin Peregrine. "What I am going to tell you about now happened in the country. It was up in the north, and in a part where Europeans had very rarely been seen."

"How came you to be there, Cousin Peregrine?"

"I was not on duty. I had got leave for a few days to go up and see Pekin. Therefore I was not in uniform, remember, but in plain clothes.

"On this particular occasion I was on the river Peiho, in one of the clumsy Chinese river-boats. If the wind were favourable, we sailed; if we went with the stream—well and good. If neither stream nor wind were in our favour, the boat was towed."

"Like a barge—with a horse—Cousin Peregrine?"

"Like a barge, Maggie, but not with a horse. One or two of the Chinamen put the rope round them and pulled us along. It was not a quick way of travelling, as you may believe, and when the Peiho was slow and winding, I got out and walked by the paths among the fields."

"Paths and fields—like ours?"

"Yes. Very like some bits of the agricultural parts of England. But no pretty meadows. Every scrap of land seemed to be cultivated for crops. You know the population of China is enormous, and the Chinese are very economical in using their land to produce food, and as they are not great meat-eaters—as we are—their fields are mostly ploughed and sown, so I walked along among rice-fields and cotton-fields, and with little villages here and there, where the cottages are built of mud or stone with tile roofs."

"Did you see any of the villagers?"

"Most certainly I did. You must know that the inhospitable way in which the Chinese and Japanese have for many long years received strangers has come from misunderstandings, and ignorance, and suspicion, and perhaps from some other reasons; but the Chinese and Japanese villagers who see strangers for the first time, and have lived quiet country lives out of the way of politics, are often very hospitable and friendly. I am bound, however, to except the women; not because they wished us ill, but they are afraid of strangers, and they kept well out of our way."

"Do the village Chinese women have those funny smashed-up feet, Cousin Peregrine?"

"In the north of China they have. In the south only ladies deform themselves in this fashion; and the Tartar women always leave their own beautiful little feet uninjured. Well, the men came out of their cottages and fields, and pressed eagerly but good-naturedly round me."

"Do the village men wear pigtails?"

"Every Chinaman wears a pigtail. A Chinaman without a pigtail would be as great a rarity as a Manx cat, or rather, I ought to say, he would be like the tailless fox in the fable; only you would never catch a Chinaman trying to persuade his friends that it was creditable to have no tail! For I must tell you that pigtails are sometimes cut off—as a degradation—when a man has committed some crime. But as soon as he can, he gets the barber to put him on a false pigtail, as a closely-cropped convict might wear a wig. They roll them up when they are at work if they are in the way, but if a servant came into your room with his tail tucked up you would be very angry with him, It would be like a housemaid coming in with her sleeves and skirt tucked up for house-cleaning—*most* disrespectful!"

"Were these the men you showed something to that *they* thought wonderful?"

"Yes, Fred. And now I'll tell you what it was. You must know that I could speak no Chinese, and my new friends could speak no English, so they chattered like magpies to each other, and laughed like children or Chinamen—for the Chinese are very fond of a joke. When they laughed I laughed, and we bowed and shook hands, and they turned me round and felt me all over, and *felt my hands*."

"What about your hands, Cousin?"

"I had on dog-skin gloves, yellow ones. Now when all the male population of the hamlet had stroked these very carefully, I perceived that they had never seen gloves before, and that they believed themselves to be testing the feel of a barbarian's skin."

"Barbarian?"

"Certainly, Bessie. They give us the same polite name that we feel ourselves more justified in applying to them. Well, when they had laughed, and I had laughed, and we had shaken hands afresh, laughing heartily as we did so, and I began to feel it was time to go on and catch up my boat, which was floating sluggishly down the winding stream of the Peiho, I resolved on one final effect, like the last scene of a dramatic performance. Making vigorous signs and noises, to intimate that something was coming, and they must look out sharp, and feeling very much like a conjurer who has requested his audience to keep their eyes on him and 'see how it's done'—I slyly unbuttoned my gloves, and then with much parade began to draw one off by the finger-tips.

"'Eyah! Eyah!' cried the Chinamen on all the notes of the gamut, as they fell back over each other. *They thought I was skinning my hands.* I 'smiled superior,' as I took the gloves off, and made an effect almost as great by putting them on again."

"Oh, Cousin Peregrine, weren't they astonished?"

"They were, Maggie, And unless they are more familiar with Europeans now, the mystery is probably to this day as unsolved to them as the trick of the ball of thread and the twelve needles still is to me. By this time, however, my boat was

'Far off, a blot upon the stream,'

and I had to hasten away as fast as I could to catch it up. I parted on the most friendly terms from my narrow-eyed acquaintance, but when I had nearly regained my boat I could still see them in their blue-cotton dresses and long pigtails, gazing open-mouthed at my vanishing figure across the rice-fields."

* * * * *

After a few seconds' silence, during which Maggie had sat with her eyes thoughtfully fixed on the fire, she said, "Cousin Peregrine, you said in your letters that it was very cold in the north of China. If Chinamen know nothing about gloves, how can they keep their hands warm?" Maggie had a little the air of regarding this question as a poser, but Cousin

Peregrine was not disconcerted.

"My dear Maggie, your question reminds me of another occasion, when I astonished a most respectable old China gentleman by my gloves. I will tell you about it, as it will show you how the Chinese keep their hands warm.

"It was on this very same expedition. We were at Tung-Chow, about eight miles from Pekin. At this place we had to leave the river, and take to our Tartar ponies, which our Chinese horse-boys had ridden up to this point to meet us. We had hired a little cart to convey our baggage, and I was sitting on my pony watching the lading up of the cart, when a dear old Chinaman, dressed in blue wadded silk, handsomely lined with fur, came up to me, and with that air of gentlemanly courtesy which is by no means confined to Europe, began to explain and expound in his own language for my benefit."

"What was he talking about? Could you tell?"

"I soon guessed. The fact is I am not very apt to wear gloves when I can help it, especially if I am working at anything. At the moment the old Chinese gentleman came up I was holding the reins of my pony with bare hands (my gloves being in my pocket), and as the morning was cold, my fingers looked rather blue. Having ascertained by feeling that my coat-sleeves would not turn down any lower than my wrists, he touched my hands softly, and made courteous signs, indicating that he was about to do me a good turn. Having signalled a polite disapprobation of the imperfect nature of my sleeves, he drew my attention to his own deep wide ones. Turning them back so as to expose the hands, the fine fur lining lay like a rich trimming above his wrists. Then with a glance of infinite triumph he bespoke my close attention as, shivering, to express cold, he turned the long sleeves, each a quarter of a yard, over his hands, and stuffing each hand into the opposite sleeve they were warm and comfortable, as it were in a muff, which was a part of his coat. More sensible than our muffs too, the fur was inside instead of out.

"He was the very pink of politeness, but at this point his pride of superior intelligence could not be restrained, and he broke into fits of delighted laughter, in which the horse-boys, the spectators, my friends, and (as is customary in China) everybody within sight and hearing joined.

"I took good care to laugh heartily too. After which I made signs the counterpart of his. He looked anxious. I put my hand in my pocket, and drew out my gloves. He stared. *I put them on*, and nodded, to show that that was the way we barbarians did it.

"'Eyah!' cried the silk-robed old gentleman."

"'Eyah!' echoed the horse-boys and the crowd."

"Then I laughed, and the horse-boys laughed loudly, and the crowd louder still, and finally the old gentleman doubled himself up in his blue silk fur-lined robe in fits of laughter."

"An Asiatic only relishes one thing better than being outwitted—that is to outwit."

"'Eyah! Eyah! Ha! ha! ha!' they cried as we rode away."

"'Ha! ha! ha!' replied I, waving a well-gloved hand, on my road to Pekin."

WAVES OF THE GREAT SOUTH SEAS

(*Founded on Fact.*)

"Very likely the man who drew it had been nearly drowned by one himself."

"Very likely nothing of the sort!"

"How could he draw it if he hadn't seen it?"

"Why, they always do. Look at Uncle Alfred, he drew a splendid picture of a shipwreck. Don't you remember his doing it at the dining-room table, and James coming in to lay the cloth, and he would have a bit of the table left clear for him, because he was in the middle of putting in the drowning men, and wanted to get them in before luncheon? And Uncle Herbert wrote a beautiful poem to it, and they were both put into a real magazine. And Uncle Alfred and Uncle Herbert never were in shipwrecks. So there!"

"Well, Uncle Alfred drew it very well, and he made very big waves. So there!"

"Ah, but he didn't make waves like a great wall. He did it very naturally, and he draws a great deal better than those rubbishy old pictures in Father's *Robinson Crusoe*."

"Well, I don't care. The Bible says that when the Children of Israel went through the Red Sea the waters were a wall to them on their right hand and on their left. And I believe they were great waves like the wave in *Robinson Crusoe*, only they weren't allowed to fall down till Pharaoh and his host came, and then they washed them all away."

"But that's a miracle. I don't believe there are waves like that now."

"I believe there are in other countries. Uncle Alfred's shipwreck was only an English shipwreck, with waves like the waves at the seaside."

"Let's ask Cousin Peregrine. He's been in foreign countries, and he's been at sea."

The point in dispute between Maggie and her brother was this:—The nursery copy of *Robinson Crusoe* was an old one which had belonged to their father, with very rough old wood-cuts, one of which represented Robinson Crusoe cowering under a huge wave, which towered far above his head, and threatened to overwhelm him. This wave Maggie had declared to be unnatural and impossible, whilst the adventure-book young gentleman clung to and defended an illustration which had helped him so vividly to realize the sea-perils of his hero.

It was the day following that of Cousin Peregrine's arrival, and when evening arrived the two children carried the book down with them to dessert, and attacked Cousin Peregrine simultaneously.

"Cousin Peregrine, you've been at sea: isn't that an impossible wave?"

"Cousin Peregrine, you've been at sea: aren't there sometimes waves like that in foreign places?"

"It's not very cleverly drawn," said Cousin Peregrine, examining the wood-cut; "but making allowance for that, I have seen waves not at all unlike this one."

"There!" cried the young gentleman triumphantly. "Maggie laughed at it, and said it was like a wall."

"Some waves are very like walls, but those are surf-waves, as they are called, that is, waves which break upon a shore. The waves I am thinking of just now are more like mountains—translucent blackish-blue mountains—mountains that look as if they were made of bottle-green glass, like the glass mountain in the fairy tale, or shining mountains of phosphorescent light—meeting you as if, they would overwhelm you, passing under you, and tossing you like the old woman in the blanket, and then running away behind you as you go to meet another. Every wave with a little running white crest on its ridge; though not quite such a curling frill as this one has which is engulfing poor Robinson Crusoe. But his is a surf-wave, of course. Those I am speaking of are waves in mid-ocean."

"Not as tall as a man, Cousin Peregrine?"

"As tall as many men piled one upon another, Maggie."

"It certainly is very funny that the children should choose this subject to tease you about tonight, Peregrine," said Mamma.

We are all apt to speak inaccurately. Mamma did not mean that the subject was a comical one, but that it was remarkable that the children should have started it at dessert, when the grown-up people had been discussing it at dinner.

They had not been talking about Robinson Crusoe's wave, but about the loss of an Australian vessel, in sad circumstances which were in every one's mouth. A few people only had been saved. They had spent many days in an open boat in great suffering, and the particular question discussed at dinner was, whether the captain of a certain vessel which had passed without rescuing them had been so inhuman as to see and yet to leave them.

"How could he help seeing them?" Mamma had indignantly asked. "It was daylight, and of course somebody was on the deck, even if the captain was still in bed. Don't talk to me, Peregrine! You would say black is white for the sake of argument, especially if it was to defend somebody. But little as I know about the sea, I know that it's flat."

"And that's flat!" interposed Papa.

"It's all very well making fun of me," Mamma had continued with good-humoured vehemence, "but there were no Welsh hills and valleys to block the view of castaway fellow-creatures not a mile off, and it was daylight, and he *must* have seen them."

"I'm not quite sure about the hills and valleys," Cousin Peregrine had replied; "and hills of water are quite as troublesome to see through as hills of earth."

At this moment the dining-room door had opened to admit the children, Maggie coming first, and making her courtesy in the doorway, with the old fat, brown-calf-bound *Robinson Crusoe* under her arm. It opened without the slightest difficulty at the picture of the big wave, and the children appealed to Cousin Peregrine as has been related.

Maggie was a little taken aback by a decision which was in favour of her brother's judgment. She was apt to think rather highly of her own, and even now she pondered, and then put another question—

"But if the waves were so very, very big, Cousin, they would swallow up the ships!"

"No, Maggie, not if the sailors manage their ship properly, and turn her about so that she meets the wave in the right way. Then she rides over it instead of being buried under it."

"It would be dreadful if they didn't!" said Maggie.

"I remember being in a ship that didn't meet one of these waves in the right way," said Cousin Peregrine.

"Tell us all about it," said Fred, settling himself with two or three severe fidgets into the seat of his chair.

"I *was* going to have protested against the children asking you for another story so soon, Peregrine," said Mamma, "but now I feel selfish, for your wave-story will be quite as much for me as for the little ones."

"Where was it, Cousin Peregrine?"

"Where was the wave, do you mean? It was in the great South Seas. As to where I was, I was in a sailing-vessel bound for South Australia. To begin at the beginning, I must explain to you that this vessel was one of those whose captains accepted the instruments offered by the Board of Trade to any ship that would keep a meteorological log. I was fond of such matters, and I took the trouble off the captain's hands, by keeping his meteorological log for him."

"What is a meteorological log, Cousin?"

"A kind of diary, in which you put down the temperature of the sea and air, how cold or hot they are—the way the wind blows, how the barometer is, and anything special and interesting about the weather overhead or the currents in the sea. Now I must tell you that there had been a good deal of talk about currents of warm water in the Southern Ocean, like the Gulf Stream of the Atlantic, which keeps the west coasts of Great Britain so warm. But these South Sea currents had not been very accurately observed, and information on the subject was desired. Well, one day we got right into a warm current."

"How did you know, Cousin?"

"By drawing up a bucket of water out of the sea, and putting the thermometer into it. But I ought to tell you what a thermometer is—"

"We know quite well," said Maggie. "Nurse always put it into Baby's bath when he had fits, to see if the water was the right warmth."

"Very good, Maggie. Then let me tell you that the water of the sea got nearly thirty degrees warmer on that day between noon and midnight."

"How did you know about midnight?" Maggie inquired doubtfully; "weren't you in bed?"

"No, I was not, I was very busy all day 'taking observations' every hour or two, and it was at twelve o'clock this very night that the 'comber' broke on deck."

"What *is* a 'comber'?"

"A 'comber' is the name for a large wave with a comb or crest of foam, a sort of wave over which our ship ought to have ridden; but I must tell you that it was no easy matter to meet them on this occasion, because (owing to the cross currents) the waves did not all go one way, but came at us from various points. The sea was very heavy, and the night was very dark. I tried the heat of the water for the last time that evening, and having bade good-night to the officer whose watch was just over, I stayed for a few minutes to talk to the officer whose watch was just beginning, before going below to go to bed. We were standing aft, and, fortunately for us, near one of the masts, when through the darkness we saw the sloping sides of a great South Sea wave coming at the fore part of the ship, but sideways. 'The rigging!' shouted the officer of the watch, and as we both clung to the ropes the wave broke on our bows, smashed the jib-boom, and swept the decks from stem to stern."

"And if you hadn't held on by the rigging you would have been washed away?"

"I am afraid we should, Fred, for every loose thing on deck was swept off in less than a minute. The bull kept his feet, by the bye; but then he had four, and I have only two."

"The bull! what bull?"

"We were taking some cattle out to Australia. There was a bull who lived in a stable that had been made for him on deck. When this comber broke over us it tore up the bull's house, and carried it overboard, but I met the bull himself taking a walk at large as I went below to change my clothes and get some sleep."

"Were you wet?"

"Drenched, my dear Maggie; but when I got to my cabin I found that there was no hope of rest for some hours. The wave had flooded the cabins, broken in doors, and washed everything and everybody about. So we all had to set to work to bale out water, and mop up our bed-rooms; and as the wave had also put out what lights there were, we had to work in the dark, and very uncomfortable work it was! What the women and children did, and the poor people who were sea-sick, I hardly know. Of course we who could keep our feet did the work."

"Weren't you ever sea-sick?"

"Never, I am thankful to say."

"Not when it's very, very rough?"

"Not in a gale. I have once or twice on that voyage been the captain's only companion at dinner, tied to the mast to keep myself steady, and with the sherry in one pocket and my wine-glass in another to keep *them* steady, and quite ashamed of my appetite, for if the sea doesn't make you feel very ill it makes you feel very well."

"I had no idea there were such very big waves really," said Maggie, thoughtfully.

"I see that they are quite big enough to shelter the captain's character, Peregrine," said Mamma, smiling, "and I am much obliged to you for correcting my ignorance. I don't *wish* to believe that any English sailor would pass a boat in distress without giving help, if he saw it."

"I am quite sure no English sailor would, and very few real sailors of any nation, I think. A real seaman knows too well what sea-perils are, and that what is another man's case one day may be his the next; and cowardice and cold-heartedness are the last sins that can be laid at Jack Tar's door as a rule. But I will finish my story by telling the children what happened next morning, as it goes to illustrate both my statements, that it is not easy to see an open boat in a heavy sea, and that sailors are very ready to risk their lives for each other."

"You're like Captain Marryat, Cousin Peregrine," said Fred.

"He's not a sailor captain, he's a soldier captain," said Maggie. "Go on, Cousin."

"As I told you, we had two or three hours of very disagreeable work before our cabins were even tolerably comfortable; but it made us more tired than ever, and when I did turn in I slept like a top, and the rolling of the ship only rocked me to sounder slumbers. I was awakened at seven o'clock next morning by a fellow-passenger, who popped in to cry, 'There's a man overboard!' 'Who?' shouted I as I jumped up. 'Giovanni,' he replied as he vanished, leaving me to follow him on deck as quickly as possible. Now, Fred, picture to yourself a grey morning, the damp deck of our vessel being rapidly crowded with everybody on board, and all eyes strained towards a heavy sea, with big blue-black mountains of water running at us, and under us, and away from us all along; every wave had a white crest: but there were some other patches of snowy white hovering over the dark sea, on which all the experienced eyes were soon fixed!"

"What were they?" whispered Fred.

"Albatross," said Cousin Peregrine. "They had been following us for days, hovering, swooping, and whirling those great white wings of theirs, which sometimes measure nine feet from tip to tip."

"What did they follow you for?"

"They came to pick up anything that may be thrown overboard, and they came now, as we knew, after poor Giovanni, whose curly black head kept ducking out of their way as he swam with desperate courage in our wake."

"Oh, Cousin Peregrine! Didn't the captain stop the ship?"

"Certainly, Maggie, though, quickly as it was done, it left the poor fellow far away behind. And heavy as the sea was, they were lowering a boat when I got on deck, and the captain had called for volunteers among the sailors to man it."

"Oh, I hope he got them!"

"I hope you won't insult a noble and gallant profession by having any doubt about it, Maggie. He might have had the ship's crew bodily if he had wanted them, and if the waves had run twice as high."

"Spare me!" said Mamma.

"As it was the few men needed were soon ready. The boat was launched without being upset, and the men got in without mishap. Then they laid themselves to their oars, we gave them a parting cheer, and they vanished from our sight."

"*Drowned*, Cousin Peregrine?"

"No, no. Though I can tell you we were as anxious for them as for Giovanni now. But when they had crossed the first water-mountains, and gone down into the water-valleys beyond, they were quite out of sight of the crowd on the deck of the ship, daylight though it was."

"I retract everything I ever said," cried Mamma impetuously.

"And not only could we not see them, but they could not see the man they were risking their lives to save. Those crested mountains which hid them from us hid him from them."

"What *did* you do?"

"Men were sent up the masts to look out from such a height that they could look over the waves. *They* could see both Giovanni and the boat, and as they were so high up the men in the boat could see them. So the men on the masts kept their eyes on Giovanni, and the men in the boat kept their eyes on the men on the masts, and steered their course according to the signals from the look-out."

"And they saved him?"

"Yes, they brought him back; and if we cheered when they went away, you may believe we cheered when they got safe to the ship's side again."

"And who was Giovanni? and did he get all right?"

"Giovanni was one of the sailors, an Italian. He was a fine young fellow, and appeared to think nothing whatever of his adventure. I remember he resolutely refused to go below and change his clothes till he had helped to haul up the boat. With his white teeth shining through a broad grin, he told us in his broken English that he had been overboard every voyage he had taken. He said he didn't mind anything except the swooping and pecking of the albatross. They obliged him to dive so constantly, to keep his eyes from their beaks."

"Was it a comber washed him overboard?"

"No. He was mending the jib-boom, and lost his hold and fell into the sea. He really had a very narrow escape. A less active swimmer might easily have been drowned. I always think, too, that he had an advantage in the fact that the water was warm."

"I am so glad the nasty albatross were disappointed."

"The nasty albatross were probably disappointed when they found that Giovanni was not a piece of spoilt pork. However, they set their beautiful wings, and went their way, and we set our sails, and went our way, which was to Adelaide, South Australia."

COUSIN PEREGRINE'S TRAVELLER'S TALES

JACK OF PERA

(*Founded on Fact.*)

"Cousin Peregrine, oughtn't we to love our neighbour, whether he's a nice neighbour or a nasty neighbour?"

"Certainly, Maggie."

"But need we when he's a nasty *next-door* neighbour?" asked Fred, in such rueful tones that Cousin Peregrine burst out laughing and said, "Who is your nasty next-door neighbour, Fred, and what has he done?"

"Well, his name is Mackinnon, Cousin; and everybody says he's always quarrelling; and he complained of our screaming and the cockatoo playing—no, of the cockatoo's screaming and our playing prisoners' base, and he kept our ball once, and now he has complained of poor dear Ponto's going into his garden, and the dear darling old thing has to be tied up, except when we take him out for stiff walks."

"I didn't notice anything stiff about his walk yesterday, Fred, He took the fence into your nasty neighbour's garden at one bound, and came back with another."

"I don't know what can make him go there!" cried Fred; "I wish he understood about keeping to his own grounds."

"Ponto never lived in Constantinople, that is evident," said Cousin Peregrine.

"Did you ever live in Constantinople, Cousin?" asked Maggie.

"Yes, Maggie, I am happy to say I have."

"Why are you glad, Cousin?"

"Because in some respects it is the loveliest city on earth, and I am glad to have seen it."

"Tell us what it is like."

"And tell us why you say Ponto never lived there."

"I was a good deal younger than I am now," said Cousin Peregrine, "when I saw Constantinople for the first time, and had seen much less of the world than I have seen since; but even now I remember nothing in my travels with greater delight than my first sight of that lovely city. It was from the sea. Do you know anything about the Sea of Marmora, Fred?"

"I don't think I know much," said Fred doubtfully.

"But we've got an atlas," said Maggie, "so you can show it us, you know."

"Well, give me the map. Here is the Sea of Marmora, with Turkey-in-Europe on one side of it, and Turkey-in-Asia on the other side of it. This narrower part that you come into it

Juliana Horatia Ewing

by is called the Dardanelles, that narrower part that you go out of it by is called the Bosphorus. The Bosphorus is about two miles broad; it is salt water, you know, and leads from the Sea of Marmora to the Black Sea, which is farther north. This narrow piece of water going westward out of the Bosphorous is called the Golden Horn. Constantinople—which is built, like Rome, on hills—rises above the shores of the Bosphorus and on both sides of the Golden Horn. The part of it which is south of the Golden Horn is called Stamboul, and is the especially Turkish Quarter. Across the Golden Horn from Stamboul lies the Quarter called Galata—the commercial port—and beyond that Pera—beautiful Pera!—the Quarter where English people live when they live at Constantinople. North of these are more suburbs, and then detached Turkish villages and gay gardens dotting the banks of the Bosphorus."

"But you lived at Pera?"

"Yes, I lived at Pera; in a house looking into the Turkish cemetery."

"Was it nice, Cousin, like our churchyard? or do the Turks do horrid things with their dead people, like those Chinese you told us about, who put them in boxes high up in the air?"

"The Turks bury their dead as we do, my dear Maggie, and they plant their graveyards with cypresses, which, standing tall and dark among the headstones of the graves, have a very picturesque effect. The cemetery in all Turkish towns is a favourite place of public resort, but I cannot say that it is kept in very nice order, as a rule. For the sake of a water-colour sketch I made in one, I was very glad that the upright headstones were tumbling about in all directions, it took away the look of stiffness and monotony; but I am bound to say that the graves looked neglected as well as picturesque.

The cemetery at Pera had too much refuse, and too many cocks, hens, and dogs in it. It looked very pretty, however, from my windows, sloping down towards the Golden Horn, beyond which I could catch a glimpse of Stamboul on the heights across the water. But I have not yet told you what Constantinople looked like when I first saw it."

"You began about the Sea of Marmora, Cousin, and here it is. I've had my middle finger on it ever since we found it, to keep the place."

"Very good, Maggie. We were coming up the Sea of Marmora one evening, and drew near to Constantinople about sunrise. I knew we were near, but I could not see anything, because a thick white mist hung in front of us like a veil resting on the sea. We were near the mouth of the Bosphorus when the sun broke out, the white mist rose slowly, like the curtain of a theatre, and—more beautiful than any scene that human hands can ever paint—I saw the Queen of Cities glittering in the sunshine."

"What made it glitter? Are the houses built of shiny stuff?"

"The houses are built of wood, but they are painted in many colours. The rounded domes of the mosques are white, and the minarets, tall, slender, and fretted, are white, with golden tops, or white and blue. I can give you no idea how beautifully the shapes of the mosques and minarets break the uniformity of the mass of houses, nor how the gay colours, the white and the gold, shone like gems against a cloudless blue sky when the mist rose. No princess in an Eastern fairy-tale ever dazzled and delighted the beholder by lifting her veil and displaying her beauty and her jewels more than my eyes were charmed when the veil was lifted from Constantinople, and I saw her lovely and sparkling in the sun."

"Are the streets very beautiful when you get into them?"

"Ah, Fred, I am sorry to say—no. They are very dirty, and very narrow. But they are picturesque, and made doubly so by the fact that in them you meet people of all nations, in every kind of dress, gay with all colours of the rainbow."

"Are there shops in the streets?"

"Most of the shops are all together in certain streets by themselves, forming what is called a Bazaar. But in the other streets there are a few, such as sweetmeat shops and coffee shops, where the old Turks go to drink thick black coffee, and smoke, and hear the news; and (if they wish it) to be shaved."

"I thought Turks wore long beards?"

"The lower-class Turks, and the country ones, and those who like to follow the old fashions, wear beards, but they have their heads shaved, and wear the turban. Most modern Turks, Government officials, and so forth, shave off their beards and whiskers, and wear short hair and a moustache, with the fez, or cloth cap. The old-fashioned dress is much the handsomest, I think, and I am sorry it is dying out."

"The poor women-Turks aren't allowed to go out, are they, Cousin Peregrine?"

"Oh yes, they are, but they have to be veiled, and so bundled up that you can not only not tell one woman from another, but they hardly look like women at all—more like unsteady balloons, or inflated sacks of different colours. They wear yellow leather boots, and no stockings. Over the boots they wear large slippers, in which they shuffle along with a gait very little less awkward than the toddle of a cramp-footed lady in China. If they are ungraceful on foot, matters are not much better when they ride. Sitting astride a donkey (for they do not use side-saddles), a Turkish lady is about as comical an object as you could wish to behold, though I have no doubt she is quite unconscious of looking anything but dignified, as she presses on to her shopping in the Bazaar, screaming to the half-naked Arab donkey-boy to urge on her steed with his stick. As the great cloak dress, in which women envelop themselves from head to foot when they go out, is all of one colour, they have this advantage over Englishwomen out shopping, that they do not look ugly from being bedizened with ill-assorted hues and frippery trimmings. In fact a mass of Turkish women, each clothed in one shade of colour, looks very like a flower-bed—a flower-bed of sole-coloured tulips without stalks!"

"The Bazaars are bigger than Charity Bazaars, I suppose," said Maggie thoughtfully; "are they as big as the Baker Street Bazaar?"

"The Bazaar of Stamboul, the Turkish Quarter of Constantinople, is almost a Quarter by itself. It takes up many, many streets, Maggie. I am sure I wish with all my heart I could take you children through it. You would think yourselves in fairy-land, or rather in some of those underground caves full of dazzling treasures such as Aladdin found himself in."

"But why, Cousin Peregrine? Do the Turks have very wonderful things in their shops?"

"I fancy, Maggie, that in no place in the world can one see such a collection of valuable merchandise gathered from all quarters of the globe. But it is not only the gold, the jewels, the ivories, the gorgeous silks and brocades, morocco leathers, and priceless furs, which make these great Eastern markets unlike ours. The common wares for everyday use are often of a much more picturesque kind than with us. There is no great beauty in an English boot-shop, but the shoe-bazaar in Stamboul is gay with slippers of all colours, embroidered with gold and silver thread, to say nothing of the ladies' yellow leather boots. A tobacconist's shop with us is interesting to none but smokers, but Turkish pipes have stems several feet long, made of various kinds of wood, and these and the amber mouth-pieces, which are often of very great value, and enriched with jewels, make the pipe-seller's wares ornamental as well as useful. Nor can our gunsmiths' shops compete for picturesqueness with the Bazaar devoted to arms, of all sorts and kinds, elaborately mounted, decorated, sheathed, and jewelled. Turkey and Persian carpets and rugs are common enough in England now, and you know how handsome they are. Turbans, and even fezes, you will allow to look prettier than English hats. Then some of the shops display things that one does not see at all at home, such as the glass lamps for hanging in the mosques and Greek churches. Nor is it the things for sale alone which make the Bazaar so wonderful a sight. The buyers and sellers are at least as picturesque as what they sell and buy. The floor of each shop is raised two or three feet from the ground, and on a gay rug the turbaned Turk who keeps it sits cross-legged and smokes his pipe and makes his bargains, whilst down the narrow street (which in many instances is arched overhead with stone) there struggle, and swarm, and scream, and fight, black slaves, obstinate camels, primitive-looking chariots full of Turkish ladies, people of all colours in all costumes, and from every part of the world."

"It must be a wonderful place," sighed Maggie; "streets full of beautiful shoes, and streets full of beautiful carpets."

"Just so, Maggie."

"Not at all like a London Bazaar, then. I thought perhaps it was a place that shut up to itself, with a beadle sitting at the door?"

"I never was in Stamboul at night, but my belief is that the Bazaar is secured at night by the locking up of gates. You know the people who own the shops do not live in them, and as most valuable merchandise remains in the Bazaar, it must be protected in some way. I suppose the watchmen look after it."

"Have the Turks watchmen like the old London watchmen, Cousin? With nightcaps, and rattles, and lanterns, and big coats?"

"The Turkish watchmen wear turbans—not nightcaps; but they have lanterns and big coats, and in one respect they are remarkably like the old 'Charlies,' as the London watchmen used to be called. Their object is not (like policemen) to find robbers and misdoers, but to frighten them away. Just as the old Charlies used to spring their wooden rattles that the thieves might get out of their way, so the Turkish watchman strikes the ground with an iron-shod staff, that makes a great noise, for the same purpose. In one respect, however, the Turkish watchmen are most useful—they give warning of fires."

"Are there often fires in Constantinople?"

"Very often, Fred. And when a big straggling city is built of wood in a hot climate which keeps the wood so dry that a spark will set it ablaze, when the water-supply is small, and the water-carriers, who feed the fire-engines from their leathern water-pots, are chiefly bent upon securing their pay for the help they give; and when, to crown all, the sufferers themselves are generally of the belief that what is to happen will happen, and that there is very little use in trying to avert calamity—you may believe that a fire, once started, spreads not by houses, but by streets, leaving acres of black ruins dotted with the still standing chimneys. However, I fancy that of late years wider streets and stone buildings are becoming commoner. There were stone houses, built by Europeans, in Constantinople even when I was there."

"Did you see a fire whilst you were there?"

"Yes, indeed. One came so near the house where I lived that I had everything packed up ready for a start, but fortunately my house escaped. I must tell you that the Turks have one very sensible custom in connection with these fires. They have what are called fire-towers, on which men are stationed to give warning when a fire breaks out in any part of the town. They have a system of signals, by which they show in what quarter of the city the fire is. At night the signalling is done by lamps. There is an old Genoese tower between Pera and Galata which has been made into a fire-tower. The one at Stamboul I think is modern. These buildings are tall—like light-houses—so that the signals can be seen from all parts of Constantinople, and so that the men stationed on them have the whole city in view. Besides these signals, it is part of the watchman's duty, as I told you, to give warning of a fire, and the quarter in which it has broken out. I assure you one listens with some anxiety when the ring of his iron-tipped staff on the rough pavement is followed by the cry, *'Yan ghun vah! Stamboul-dah'* ('There is a fire! In Stamboul'); or *'Yan ghun vah! Pera-dah'* ('There is a fire! In Pera')."

"But there are fire-engines?"

"There may be very good ones now. In my time nothing could be more futile than the trumpery one which was carried on men's shoulders. Indeed, until the streets are much less rough, narrow, and steep, I do not see how one could be *driven* at any speed."

"Did the men who carried the engine run?"

"Yes, and at a good swinging pace too, their half-naked bodies streaming with perspiration, and (I should have thought) their labours quite doubled by yelling as they ran. Their cries are echoed by the formidable-looking band which follows, waving long poles armed with hooks, &c., for pulling down houses to stop the progress of the flames. On the heels of these figures follow mounted officials, whose dignity is in a fixed proportion to the extent of the calamity. If the fire is a very very extensive one, the Sultan himself has to be upon the spot."

"It must be very exciting," said Fred, in a tone of relish.

"You've told us lots about Constantinople now, Cousin Peregrine," said Maggie, who had the air of having heard quite enough on the subject; "now tell us about why you said Ponto never was in Constantinople. Don't the Turks keep dogs?"

"Not as we do, for pets and friends; and yet the dog population of Constantinople is more numerous and powerful, and infinitely more noisy, than I can easily describe to you."

"Whom do they belong to then?"

"They have no special masters or mistresses. They are more like troops of wolves than a collection of Pontos."

"But who gives them their dinners?"

"They live on offal and the offscourings of the city, and though the Turks freely throw all their refuse into their streets, there are so many dogs that they are all half-starved. They are very fierce, and have as a rule a great dislike to strangers. At night they roam about the streets, and are said to fall upon any one who does not carry a lantern."

"But does anybody carry a lantern—except the watchmen?"

"Everybody does. Coloured paper lanterns, like the Chinese ones, with a bit of candle inside. With one of these in one hand and a heavy stone or stick in the other, you may get safely through a night-walk among the howling dogs of Stamboul."

"What horrible beasts!"

"I think you would pity them if you were there. They are half starved, and have no friends."

"There isn't a home for lost and starving dogs in Constantinople then?"

"The whole city may be considered as the headquarters of starving dogs, but not of lost ones. That reminds me why I said Ponto had not lived there. If he had he would know his own grounds, and keep to them."

"But, Cousin Peregrine, I thought you said the Turkish dogs had no particular homes?"

"Every dog in Constantinople belongs to a particular Quarter of the town, which he knows, and to which he confines himself with marvellous sagacity. In the Quarter in which he was born, there he must live, and there (if he wishes to die peaceably) he must die. If he strays on any pretext into another Quarter, the dogs of the Quarter he has invaded will tear him to pieces, and dine upon his bones."

"How does he know where his own part of the town begins and ends?"

"I cannot tell you, Maggie. But I can tell you of my own knowledge that he does. Jack did, though we tried to deceive him over and over again."

"Who was Jack?"

"The handsomest dog I ever saw in Constantinople. The Turkish dogs are by no means beautiful as a rule, they are too much like jackals, and as they are apt to be maimed and covered with scars from fights with each other, they do not make much of what good looks they have. However, Jack was rather less wild and wolfish-looking than most of his friends. He was of a fine tawny yellow, and had an intelligent face, poor fellow. He belonged to our Quarter—in fact the cemetery was his home till he took to lying at our door."

"Then he was a Pera dog?"

"Yes, and I and the brother-officers who were living with me made friends with him. We gave him food and spoke kindly to him, and he laid aside his prejudices against foreigners, and laid his tawny limbs on our threshold. We became really attached to each other. He received the very British name of Jack, and seemed quite contented with it. He took walks with us. It was then that again and again we tried to deceive him about the limits of his Quarter, and get him into another one unawares. He never was misled. But later on, as he grew tame, less fearful of things in general, and more unwilling to quit us when we were out together, he sometimes strayed beyond his bounds, not because he was deceived as to his limits, but he ventured on the risk for our sakes. Even then, however, he would not walk in the public thoroughfares, he 'dodged' through gardens, empty courtyards and quiet by-places where he was not likely to meet the outraged dogs of the Quarter he was invading. The moment we were safe back 'in bounds' he came freely and happily to our side once more. I have often wondered, since I left Constantinople, how long Jack lived, and how he died."

"Oh, didn't you take him away?"

"I couldn't, my dear. And you must not think, Maggie, that if Turks do not pet dogs they are cruel to them. It is not the case. A Turk would never dream of petting a dog, but if he saw one looking hot and thirsty in the street he would be more likely to take trouble to get it a dish of water than many English people who feed their own particular pets on mutton-chops. Jack was not likely to be ill-treated after our departure, but I sometimes have a heart-sore suspicion that we may have raised dreams in his doggish heart never again to be realized. If he were at all like other dogs (and the more we knew of him the more companionable he became), he must have waited many a long hour in patient faithfulness at our deserted threshold. He must have felt his own importance as a dog with a name, in that wild and nameless tribe to which he belonged. He must have dreamed of his foreign friends on many a blazing summer's afternoon. Perhaps he stole cautiously into other Quarters to look for us. I hope he did not venture too far—Maggie—my dear Maggie! You are not fretting about poor Jack? I assure you that really the most probable thing is that our successors made friends with him."

"Do you really and truly think so, Cousin Peregrine?"

"On my word of honour I do, Maggie. You must remember that Jack was not a Stamboul dog. He belonged to Pera, where Europeans live, so there is a strong probability that his unusual tameness and beauty won other friends for him when we had gone."

"I hope somebody very nice lived in your house when you went away."

"I hope so, Maggie."

"Cousin Peregrine, do you think we could teach Ponto to know his own quarter?"

"I think you could, Fred. I once lived next door to a man who was very fond of his garden. It was a mere strip in front of his hut—for we were quartered in camp at this time—and not even a paling separated it from a similar strip in front of my quarters. My bit, I regret to say, was not like his in any respect but shape. I had a rather ragged bit of turf, and he had a glowing mass of flowers. The monotony of my grass-plat was only broken by the marrow-bones and beef-ribs which my dog first picked and then played with under my windows. I was as fond of him as my brother-officer was of his flowers. I am sorry to say that Dash had a fancy for the gayer garden, and for some time my good-tempered neighbour bore patiently with his inroads, and with a sigh buried the beef-bone that Dash had picked among the mignonette at the roots of a magnificent rose which he often alluded to as 'John Hopper,' and seemed to treat as a friend. Mr. Hopper certainly throve on Dash's bones, but unfortunately Dash took to applying them himself to the roots of plants for which I believe that bone manure is not recommended. When he made a hole two foot deep in the Nemophila bed, and laid a sheep's head by in it against a rainy day, I felt that something must be done. After the humblest apologies to my neighbour, I begged for a few days' grace. He could not have spoken more feelingly of the form, scent, and colour of his friend John Hopper than I ventured to do in favour of the intelligence of my friend Dash. In short I begged for a week's patience on his part, that I might teach Dash to know his own garden. If I failed to do so, I promised to put him on the chain, much as I dislike tying up dogs."

"How did you manage, Cousin?"

"Whenever Dash strayed into the next garden, I began to scold him in the plainest English, and covered him with reproaches, till he slunk gradually back to his own untidy grass-plat. When he touched his own grounds, I changed my tone at once, to approbation. At first this change simply brought him flying to my feet again, if I was standing with my friend in his garden. But after a plentiful application of, 'How dare you, Sir? Go back' (pointing), 'go back to your garden. If this gentleman catches you here again, he'll grind your bones to make John Hopper's bread. That's a good dog. No! Down! Stay where you are!'—Dash began to understand. It took many a wistful gaze of his brown eyes before he fully comprehended what I meant, but he learned it at last. He never put paw into Major E—'s garden without looking thoroughly ashamed of himself. He would lie on his own ragged lawn and wistfully watch me sitting and smoking among the roses; but when I returned to our own quarters he welcomed me with an extravagant delight which seemed to congratulate me on my escape from the enemy's country."

"Oh, Cousin Peregrine! We must try and teach Ponto to know his own garden."

"I strongly advise you to do so. Ponto is a gentleman of honour and intelligence, I feel convinced. I think he will learn his neighbourly duties, and if he does do so as well as Dash did—whatever you may think of Mr. Mackinnon—I think Mr. Mackinnon will soon cease to regard Ponto as—a nasty next-door neighbour."

THE PRINCES OF VEGETATION

This fanciful and high-sounding title was given by the great Swedish botanist, Linnaeus, to a race of plants which are in reality by no means distantly allied to a very humble family—the family of Rushes.

The great race of Palms puzzled the learned Swede. He did not know where to put them in his system; so he gave them an appendix all to themselves, and called them the Princes of Vegetation.

The appendix cannot have been a small one, for the Order of Palms is very large. About five hundred different species are known and named, but there are probably many more.

They are a very beautiful order of plants; indeed, the striking elegance of their forms has secured them a prominence in pictures, poetry, and proverbs, which makes them little less familiar to those who live in countries too cold for them to grow in, than to those whose home, like theirs, is in the tropics. The name Palm (Latin, *Palma*) is supposed to have been applied to them from a likeness in the growth of their branches to the outspread palm of the hand; and the fronds of some of the fan-palms are certainly not unlike the human hand, as commonly drawn by street-boys upon doors and walls.

Juliana Horatia Ewing

So beautiful a tree, when it flourished in the symbol-loving East, was sure to be invested with poetical and emblematical significance. Conquerors were crowned with wreaths of palm, which is said to have been chosen as a symbol of victory, because of the elasticity with which it rises after the pressure of the heaviest weight—an explanation, perhaps, more appropriate to it as the emblem of spiritual triumphs—the Palm of Martyrdom and the Palms of the Blessed.

But as a religious symbol it is not confined to the Church triumphant. Not only is the "great multitude which no man can number" represented to us as "clothed in white robes, and palms in their hands"—the word "palmer" records the fact that he who returned from a pilgrimage to the Holy Land was known, not only by the cockle-shell on his gown, but by the staff of palm on which he leant. St. Gregory also alludes to the palm-tree as an accepted emblem of the life of the righteous, and adds that it may well be so, since it is rough and bare below, and expands above into greenness and beauty.

The palm here alluded to is evidently the date palm (*Phoenix dactylifera*). This is pre-eminently the palm-tree of the Bible, and was in ancient times abundant in the Holy Land, though, curiously enough, it is now comparatively rare. Jericho was known as "the city of palm-trees" in the time of Moses (Deut. xxxiv. 3). It is alluded to again in the times of the Judges (Judges i. 11; iii. 13), and it bore the same title in the days of Ahaz (2 Chron. xxviii. 15). Josephus speaks of it as still famous for its palm-groves in his day, but it is said that a few years ago only one tree remained, which is now gone.

It was under a palm that Deborah the prophetess sat when all Israel came up to her for judgment; and to an audience under the shadow of this tree, which bore her name, that she summoned Barak out of Kedesh-naphtali. Bethany means "the House of Dates," and the branches of palm which the crowd cut down to strew before our Lord as He rode into Jerusalem were no doubt of this particular species.

Women—as well as places—were often named after the Princes of Vegetation, whose graceful and stately forms approved them to lovers and poets as fit types of feminine beauty.

Usefulness, however, even more than ornament, is the marked characteristic of the tribe. "From this order (*Palmae*)," says one writer, "are obtained wine, oil, wax, flour, sugar, salt, thread, utensils, weapons, habitations, and food"—a goodly list of the necessaries of life, to which one may add many smaller uses, such as that of "vegetable ivory" for a variety of purposes, and the materials for walking-sticks, canework, marine soap, &c., &c.

The Princes of Vegetation are to be found in all parts of the world where the climate is adapted to the tropical tastes of their Royal Highnesses.

They have come into our art, our literature, and our familiar knowledge from the East; but they abound in the tropics of the West, and some species are now common in South America whose original home was in India.

The cocoa-nut palm (*Cocos nucifera*) is an Indian and South Sea Islands Prince; but his sway extends now over all tropical countries. The cocoa-nut palm begins to bear fruit in from seven to eight years after planting, and it bears on for no less than seventy to eighty years.

Length of days, you see, as well as beauty and beneficence, mark this royal race which Linnaeus placed alone!

Cocoa-nuts are useful in many ways. The milk is pleasant, and in hot and thirsty countries is no doubt often a great boon. The white flesh—a familiar school-boy dainty—is eaten raw and cooked. It produces oil, and is used in the manufacture of stearine candles. It is also used to make *marine soap*, which will lather in salt water. The wood of the palm is used for ornamental joinery, the leaves for thatch and basket-work, the fibre for cordage and cocoa-nut matting, and the husk for fuel and brushes.

Cocoa and chocolate come from another palm (*Theobroma cacao*), which is cultivated largely in South America and the West Indies.

Sago and tapioca are made from the starch yielded by several species of palm. The little round balls of sago are formed from a white powder (sago flour, as it is called), just as homoeopathic pillules are formed from sugar. It is possible to see chemists make pills from boluses to globules, but the Malay Indians are said jealously to keep the process of "pearling" sago a trade secret. Tapioca is only another form of sago starch. Sago flour is now imported into England in considerable quantities. It is used for "dressing" calicoes.

Among those products of the palm which we import most liberally is "vegetable ivory."

Vegetable ivory is the kernel of the fruit of one of the most beautiful of palms (*Phytelephas macrocarpa*).

This Prince of Vegetation is a native of South America. "It is short-stemmed and procumbent, but has a magnificent crown of light green ostrich-feather-like leaves, which rise from thirty to forty feet high." The fruit is as big as a man's head. Two or three millions of the nuts are imported by us every year, and applied to all the purposes of use and ornament for which real ivory is available.

The Coquilla-nut palm (*Attalea funifera*), whose fruit is about the size of an ostrich-egg, also supplies a kind of vegetable ivory.

Our ideas of palm-trees are so much derived from the date palm of Judaea, that an erect and stately growth is probably inseparably connected in our minds with the Princes of Vegetation. But some of the most beautiful are short-stemmed and creeping; whilst others fling giant arms from tree to tree of the tropical forests, now drooping to the ground, and then climbing up again in very luxuriance of growth. Many of the rattan palms (*Calamus*) are of this character. They wind in and out, hanging in festoons from the branches, on which they lean in princely condescension, with stems upwards of a thousand feet in length.

There is something comical in having to add that these clinging rattan stems, which cannot support their own weight, have a proverbial fame, and are in great request for the manufacture of walking-sticks. They are also largely imported into Great Britain for canework.

Another very striking genus (*Astrocaryum*) is remarkable for being clothed in every part—stem, leaves, and spathe—with sharp spines, which are sometimes twelve inches long. *Astrocaryum murumura* is edible. The pulp of the fruit is said to be like that of a melon, and it has a musky odour. It is a native of tropical America, and abundant on the Amazon. Cattle wander about the forests in search of it, and pigs fatten on the nut, which they crunch with their teeth, though it is exceedingly hard.

The date palm yields a wine called toddy, or palm wine, and from the Princes of Vegetation is also distilled a strong spirit called arrack.

And speaking again of the Judaean palms, I must here say a word of those which we associate with Palm Sunday—the willow palms—for which we used to hunt when we were children.

It is hardly necessary to state that these willow branches, with their soft silvery catkins, the crown of the earliest spring nosegays which the hedges afford, are not even distantly related to the Princes of Vegetation, though we call them palms. They are called palms simply from having taken the place of real palm-branches in the ceremonies of the Sunday of our Lord's Entry into Jerusalem, where these do not grow.

A very old writer, speaking of the Jews strewing palm-branches before Christ, says: "And thus we take palm and flowers in procession as they did ... in the worship and mind of Him that was done on the cross, worshipping and welcoming Him with song into the Church, as the people did our Lord into the city of Jerusalem. It is called Palm Sunday for because the palm betokeneth victory; wherefore all Christian people should bear palm in procession, in token that He hath foughten with the fiend our enemy, and hath the victory of hym."

A curious old Scotch custom is recorded in Lanark, as "kept by the boys of the Grammar-school, beyond all memory in regard to date, on the Saturday before Palm Sunday. They then parade the streets with a palm, or its substitute, a large tree of the willow kind (*Salix caprea*), in blossom, ornamented with daffodils, mezereon, and box-tree. This day is called Palm Saturday, and the custom is certainly a popish relic of very ancient standing."

But to return to palms proper. Before taking leave of them,

there is one more word to be said in their praise which may endear this noble race to eyes which will never be permitted to see the wonders of tropical forests.

As pot-plants they are not less remarkable for the picturesqueness of their forms, than for the patience with which they endure those vicissitudes of stuffiness and chill, dryness, dust, and gas, which prove fatal to so many inmates of the flower-stand or the window-sill. Pot-palms may be bought of any good nurseryman at prices varying from two or three shillings to two or three pounds. *Latania borbonica* and *Phoenix reclinata* are good and cheap. Sandy-peaty soil, with a little leaf-mould, is what they like, and this should be renewed (with a larger pot) every second year. Thus, with the most moderate care, and an occasional sponging, or a stand-out in a soft shower, the exiled Princes of Vegetation, whose shoots in their native forests would have been of giant luxuriance, will live for years, patiently adapting themselves by slow growth to the rooms which they adorn, easier of management than the next fern you dig up on your rambles, and, in the incomparable beauty of their forms, the perpetual delight of an artistic eye.

LITTLE WOODS

By little woods are here meant—not woods of small extent, but—woods in which the trees never grow big, woods that are to grown-up woods as children to grown-up people, woods that seem made on purpose for children, and dwarfs, and dolls, and fairies.

These little woods have many names, varying with the trees of which they are composed, or the districts in which they are found. One of the best-known names is that of copse or coppice, and it brings with it remembrances of the fresh beauty of spring days, on which—sheltered by the light copse-wood from winds that are still keen—we have revelled in sunshine warm enough to persuade us that summer was come "for good," as we picked violets and primroses to the tolling of the cuckoo.

Things "in miniature" have a natural charm for little people, and most of my young readers have probably been familiar with favourite copses, or miniature pine-forests. Perhaps some of them would like to know why these little woods never grow into big ones, and something also of the history and uses of those trees of which little woods are composed.

They are not made of dwarf trees. There are little woods, as well as big woods, of oak, elm, ash, pine, willow, birch, beech, and larch. In some cases the little woods are composed of the growth which shoots up when the principal trunk of the tree has been cut down, but they are generally little merely because they are young, and are cut down for use before they have time to grow into forest-trees. The object of this little paper is to give some account of their growth and uses. It will be convenient to take them alphabetically, by their English names.

The Ash (*Fraxinus excelsior* and other varieties) is a particularly graceful and fine tree at its full growth. It is a native of Great Britain, and of many other parts of the world. It is long lived. The most profitable age for felling it as a forest-tree is from eighty to a hundred years. The flower comes out before the leaves, which are late, like those of the oak. The bunches of seed-vessels, or "ash-keys," as they are fancifully called, were pickled in salt and water and eaten in old times. The Greeks and Romans made their spears of ash-wood. The wood is not so durable as that of some other trees, but it is tough, and is thus employed for work subject to sudden strains. It is good for kitchen-tables, as it scours well and does not easily splinter.

In little woods, or ash-holts, or ash-coppices, the ash is very valuable. They are either cut over entirely at certain intervals, or divided into portions which are cut yearly in succession. At four or five years old the ash makes good walking-sticks, crates to pack glass and china in, hoops, basket handles, fences, and hurdles. Croquet-mallets are also made of ash. At twelve or fourteen it is strong enough for hop-poles. There are many old superstitions in connection with the ash, and there is a midland counties saying that if there are no keys on the ash, within a twelvemonth there will be no king.

There are several fine American varieties, and both in the

States and in Canada the wood is used for purposes similar to ours.

The Alder (*Alnus glutinosa*, &c.) is never a very large tree. It is supposed to be in maturity when it is sixty years old. It will grow in wetter places than any other tree in Europe— even than the willow. Though the wood is soft, it is very durable in water. Virgil speaks of it as being used for boats. It is highly valued in Holland for piles, and it is said that the famous bridge of the Rialto at Venice is built on piles of alder-wood. Though invaluable for water-pipes, pump-barrels, foundations for bridges, &c., alder-wood is of little use on dry land unless it can be kept *perfectly* dry. Wooden vessels and sabots, however, are made of it.

Alders are chiefly grown in little woods. Planted by the side of rivers, too, their tough and creeping roots bind and support the banks. Alder-coppices are very valuable to the makers of—gunpowder! Every five or six years the little alders are cut down and burned to charcoal, and the charcoal of alder-wood is reckoned particularly good by gunpowder manufacturers.

The Aspen, or Trembling Poplar (*Populus tremula*), like the alder, is fond of damp situations. It has also a white soft wood, used by the turner and engraver, and for such small articles as clogs, butchers' trays, &c, &c.

The quivering of its leaves is a favourite topic with poets, and there is a curious old Highland superstition that the Cross of Christ was made of aspen-wood, and that thenceforward the tree could never rest.

In "little woods" it may be cut every seven or eight years for faggots, and at fifteen or twenty years old for poles.

The Beech (*Fagus sylvatica*). With this beautiful tree all our young readers must be familiar. There may be those whose minds are not quite clear about wych-elms and sycamores, but the appearance of the beech-tree is too strongly marked to allow of any confusion on the subject.

The beech is spoken of by Greek and Roman writers, and old writers on British agriculture count it among the four timber trees indigenous to England: the beech, the oak, the ash, and the elm.

It is said, however, not to be a native of Scotland or Ireland. It attains its full growth in from sixty to eighty years, but is believed to live to be as old as two hundred. The timber is not so valuable as that of the other three British trees, but it is used for a great variety of purposes. Like the alder, it will bear the action of water well, and has thus been used for piles, flood-gates, mill-wheels, &c. It is largely used by cabinet-makers for house furniture. It is employed also by carriage-makers and turners, and for various small articles, from rolling-pins to croquet-balls. The dried leaves are used in Switzerland to fill beds with, and very nice such beds must be! Long ago they were used for this purpose in England. Evelyn says that they remain sweet and elastic for seven or eight years, by which time a straw mattress would have become hard and musty. They have a pleasant restorative scent, something like that of green tea. When we think how many poor people lie on musty mattresses, or have none at all, whilst the beech-leaves lie in the woods and go very slowly to decay, we see one more of the many instances of people remaining uncomfortable when they need not be so, because of their ignorance. The fact that beech-leaves are very slow to rot makes them useful in the garden for mulching and protecting plants from frost.

In Scotland the beech-chips and branches are burned to

smoke herrings, and pyroligneous acid (a form of which is probably known to any of our young readers who suffer from toothache as *creosote*!) is distilled from them. Mr. Loudon tells us that the word "book" comes from the German word *buch*, which, in the first instance, means a beech, and was applied to books because the old German bookbinders used beech-wood instead of paste-board for the sides of thick volumes. Beech-wood is especially good for fuel. Only the sycamore, the Scotch pine, and the ash give out more heat and light when they burn. Beech-nuts—or beech-mast, as it is called—are eaten by many animals. Pigs, deer, poultry, &c., are turned into beech-woods to fatten on the mast. Squirrels and dormice delight in it. In France it is used to make beech-oil. This oil is used both for cooking and burning, and for the latter purpose has the valuable property of having no nasty smell.

Of the beauty of the beech as a forest-tree—let artists rave! Its smooth and shapely bole does not tempt the sketcher's eye alone. To the lover and the school-boy (and, alas! to that inartistic animal the British holiday-maker) it offers an irresistible surface for cutting names and dates. Upon its branches and beneath its shadow grow many *fungi*, several of which are eatable. Truffles are found there; those underground dainties which dogs (and sometimes pigs!) are trained to grub up for our benefit. They discover the whereabouts of the truffle by scent, for there is no sign of it above ground. Nothing else will grow under beech-trees, except holly.

Scarcely less charming than the beech-forests are beech-hedges. They cut and thrive with cutting like yew-hedges.

"Little woods" of beech are common in Buckinghamshire. They are chiefly grown for the charcoal, which is valuable for gunpowder.

"Copper-Beeches"—red-leaved beech-trees, very beautiful for ornamental purposes—all come from one red-leaved beech, a sort of freak of nature, which was found about a century ago in a wood in Germany.

The Birch (*Betula alba*, &c.) is also a tree of very distinctive appearance. The silver-white bark, which peels so delightfully under childish fingers, is not less charming to the sketcher's eye, whether as a near study or as gleaming points of high light against the grey greens and misty purples of a Highland hillside. It is emphatically the tree of the Highlands of the North. It bends and breaks not under the wildest winds, it thrives on poor soil, and defies mist and cold. So varied are its uses that it has been said that the Scotch Highlander makes everything of birch, from houses to candles, and beds to ropes! The North American Indians and the Laplanders apply it almost as universally as the Chinese use paper. The wigwams or huts of the North American Indians are made of birch-bark laid over a framework of birch-poles or trunks, and their canoes or boats are cased in it. The Laplander makes his great-coat of it,—a circular *poncho* with a hole for his head,—as well as his houses and his boots and shoes. It will be easily believed that birch-bark was used in ancient times for writing on before the invention of paper.

Birch-wood makes good fuel. It is also used by cabinet-makers. Its uses in "little woods" are many. The charcoal is good for gunpowder, and it is that of which *crayons* are made. Birch-coppices are cut for brooms, hoops, &c., at five to six years old, and at ten to twelve for faggot-wood, poles, fencing, and bark for the tanners. Birch-spray (that is, the twigs and leaves) is used for smoking hams and herrings, and for brooms to sweep grass. It is also used to make birch-rods; but as we think very ill of the discipline of any household in which the children and the pets cannot be kept in order without being beaten, we hope our own young readers are only familiar with birch-rods in picture-books.

The (Sweet or Spanish) Chestnut (*Castanca vesca*) is grown in "little woods" for hop-poles, fence-wood, and hoops. The wood of the full-grown tree is also valuable.

Evelyn says, "A decoction of the rind of the tree tinctures hair of a golden colour, esteemed a beauty in some countries." It would be entertaining to know if this is the foundation of the "auricomous fluids" advertised by hair-dressers!

Amongst "little woods" the dearest of all to the school-boy must surely be the hazel-copse! The Hazel (*Corylus avellana*) is never a large tree. It is, however, long lived, and of luxuriant growth. When cut it "stoles" or throws up shoots very freely, and when treated so will live a hundred years. With a single stem, Mr. Loudon assures us, it would live much longer. Filbert-hazels are a variety with longer nuts. Hazels are cultivated not only for the nuts, but for corf-rods,[1] hoops, fencing, &c., and hazel-charcoal, like beech-charcoal, is used for crayons. Like many other plants, the hazel has two kinds of flowers, which come out before the leaves. The long pale catkins appear first, and a little later tiny crimson flowers come where the nuts are afterwards to be.

Many old superstitions are connected with the hazel. Hazel-rods were used to "divine" for water and minerals by professors of an art which received the crack-jaw title of Rhabdomancy. Having tried our own hand at Rhabdomancy, we are able to say that the freaks of the divining-rod in sensitive fingers are sometimes as curious as those of a table among table-turners; and are probably susceptible of similar explanations.

The Larch (*Larix Europaea*, &c.). Though traceable in England for two hundred years, it is within this century that the larch has been extensively cultivated for profit. The exact date of its introduction from the mountain ranges of some other part of Europe is not known, but there is a popular tradition that it was first brought to Scotland with some orange-trees from Italy, and having begun to wither under hot-house treatment, was thrown outside, where it took root and throve thereafter. The wood of full-grown larch-trees is very valuable. To John, Duke of Athol, Scotland is indebted for the introduction of larch plantations on an enormous scale. He is said to have planted 6500 acres of mountain-ground with these valuable trees, which not only bring in heavy returns as timber, but so enrich the ground on which they grow, by the decayed *spicula* or spines which fall from them, as to increase its value in the course of some years eight or tenfold. The Duke was buried in a coffin made of larch-wood! This sounds as if the merits of the larch-tree had been indeed a hobby with him, but when one comes to enumerate them one does not wonder that a man should feel his life very usefully devoted to establishing so valuable a tree in his native country, and that the pains and pride it brought him should have awakened sentiment enough to make him desire to make his last cradle from his favourite tree.

Larch-wood is light, strong, and durable. It is used for beams and for ship-building, for railroad-sleepers and mill-axles, for water-pipes, and for panels for pictures. Evelyn says that Raphael, the great painter, painted many of his pictures on larch-wood. It will stand in heat and wet, under water and above ground. It yields good turpentine, but trees that have been tapped to procure this are of no use afterwards for building purposes. The larch is said not to make good masts for ships, but its durability in all varieties of temperature and changes of weather make it valuable for vine-props. When made of larch-poles these are never taken up as hop-poles are. Year after year the vines climb them and fade at their feet, and they are said to have outlasted at least one generation of vine-growers.

In "little woods" the larches are planted very close, so that they may "spindle up" and become tall before they grow thick. They are then used for hop-poles and props of various kinds.

The Oak (*Quercus robur*, &c.) is pre-eminently a British tree. Of its beauty, size, the venerable age it will attain, and its historical associations, we have no space to speak here, and our young readers are probably not ignorant on the subject.

The durability of its wood is proverbial. The bark is also of great value, and though the slow growth of the oak in its earlier years postpones profit to the planter, it does so little harm to other wood grown with it (being in this respect very different from the beech), that profitable coppice-wood and other trees may be grown in the same plantation.

The age at which the oak should be felled for ship-timber, &c., depends on many circumstances, and is fixed by different authorities at from eighty to a hundred and fifty years.

Oaks are said to be more liable than other trees to be struck by lightning.

Oak-coppices or "little woods" are cut over at from twelve to thirty years old. The bark is valuable as well as the wood.

The Pine (*Pinus sylvestris*, &c.), like the larch, will flourish on poor soils. It is valuable as a protection for other trees. The varieties and variations of this tree are very numerous.

It is a very valuable timber-tree, the wood being loosely known as "deal"; but "deals" are, properly speaking, planks of pine-wood of a certain thickness, "boards" being the technical name for a thicker kind. Pine trunks are used for the masts of ships. "In the north of Russia and in Lapland the outer bark is used, like that of the birch, for covering huts, for lining them inside, and as a substitute for cork for floating the nets of fishermen; and the inner bark is woven into mats like those made from the lime-tree. Ropes are also made from the bark, which are said to be very strong and elastic, and are generally used by the fishermen."

In the north of Europe great quantities of tar are procured from the Scotch pine. Torches are made from the roots and trunk.

Varieties of the pine are grown in "little woods" for hop-poles.

Pinus sylvestris (the "Scotch Pine"), though a native of Scotland, has only been planted and cultivated in Great Britain for about a century.

On the subject of "thinning and pruning" in plantations planters—like doctors—differ. An amusing story was sent to Mr. Loudon by the Duke of Bedford, in reference to his grandfather, who was an advocate for vigorous thinning in the pine plantations.

"The Duke perceived that the plantation required thinning, in order to admit a free circulation of air, and give health and vigour to the young trees. He accordingly gave instructions to his gardener, and directed him as to the mode and extent of the thinning required. The gardener paused and hesitated, and at length said: 'Your Grace must pardon me if I humbly remonstrate against your orders, but I cannot possibly do what you desire; it would at once destroy the young plantation; and, moreover, it would be seriously injurious to my reputation as a planter.' My grandfather, who was of an impetuous and decided character, but always just, instantly replied, 'Do as I desire you, and I will take care of your reputation.' The plantation was accordingly thinned according to the instructions of the Duke, who caused a board to be fixed in the plantation, facing the wood, on which was inscribed, '*This plantation has been thinned by John, Duke of Bedford, contrary to the advice and opinion of his gardener.*'"

The Willow (*Salix caprea*, &c.). The species of willow are so numerous that we shall not attempt to give a list of them.

Willow-wood wears well in water, and has been used in shipbuilding and carpentery, and especially for small ware, cricket-bats and toys. Full-grown willows of all kinds are picturesque and very graceful trees. The growth of the tree kinds when young is very rapid.

Willows are largely cultivated in "little woods" for basket-making, hoops, &c. Shoots of the *Salix caprea* of only a year's growth are large enough to be valuable for wicker-work. It appears to be held by cultivators that the poorer the soil in which they are grown the oftener these willows should be cut over. "In a good soil a coppice of this species will produce the greatest return in poles, hoops, and rods every five, six, seven, or eight years; and in middling soil, where it is grown chiefly for faggot-wood, it will produce the greatest return every three, four, or five years."

Horses and cattle are fed on the leaves of the willow in some parts of France.

Willows are often "pollarded." That is, their tops are cut off, which makes a large crop of young shoots spring out, giving a shock-headed effect which in gnarled old pollards by river-banks is picturesque enough.

The "little woods" of willow on the river Thames and the Cam are well known. They are small islands planted entirely with willows, and are called osier-holts.

Osier-beds of all kinds are very attractive "little woods." One always fancies one ought to be able to make something of the long pliable "sally-withys"—as the Wiltshire folk call willow switches. Indeed, as a matter of fact, the making of rough garden-baskets is a very simple art, especially on the Scotch and German system. Let any ingenious little prowler in an osier-bed get two thickish willow-rods and fasten them at the ends with a bit of wire, so as to make two hoops. These hoops are then to intersect each other half-way up, one being perpendicular, to form the handle and the bottom of the basket, the other being placed horizontally, to form the rim. More wire will be needed to fix them in their positions. Much finer willow-wands are used to wattle, or weave, the basket-work; ribs of split osiers are added, and the wattling goes in and out among them, and at once secures them and rests upon them.

This account is not likely to be enough to teach the most intelligent of our readers! But one fancies that a rough sort of basket-making might almost be devised out of one's own head, especially if he had been taught (as we were, by a favourite nursemaid) to plait rushes.

FOOTNOTES:

[Footnote 1: A corf is a large basket used for carrying coals or other minerals in a mine.]

MAY-DAY,

OLD STYLE AND NEW STYLE

"Now the bright morning star, day's harbinger,
Comes dancing from the East, and leads with her
The flow'ry May, who from her green lap throws
The yellow cowslip and the pale primrose."

—Milton

On the whole, perhaps, May is the most beautiful of the English months, especially the latter half of it; and yet I suppose very few May-days come round on which we are not disposed to wonder why our ancestors did not choose a warmer, and indeed a more flowery season for Maypoles and garlands and out-door festivities.

Children who live in the north of England especially must have a painfully large proportion of disappointments out of the few May-days of childhood.

Books and pictures, old stories told by Papa or Mamma of clattering chimney-sweeps and dancing May Queens, such as they saw in their young days, or heard of from their elders, have perhaps roused in us two of the strongest passions of childhood—the love of imitation and the love of flowers. We are determined to have a May-bush round the nursery-window, duly gathered before sunrise. "Pretty Bessy," our nursemaid, can do anything with flowers, from a cowslip ball to a growing forget-me-not garland. The girls are apt pupils, and pride themselves on their birthday wreaths. The boys are admirably adapted for May sweeps. Clatter is melodious in their ears. They would rather be black than white. Burnt cork will disguise them effectually; but they would prefer soot. A pole is forthcoming; ribbons are not wanting; the poodle will dance with the best of us. We have a whole holiday on Saints' Days, and the 1st of May is SS. Philip and James'.

What then hinders our enjoyment, and makes it impossible to keep May-day according to our hopes?

Too often this. It is "too cold to dawdle about." Flowers are by no means plentiful; they are pinched by the east wind. The May Queen would have to dance in her winter clothes, and would probably catch cold even then. It is not improbable that it will rain, and it is possible that it may snow. Worse than all, the hawthorn-trees are behind time, and are as obstinate as the head-nurse in not thinking the weather fit for coming out. The May is not in blossom on May-day.

And yet May-day used to be kept in the north of England as well as in warmer nooks and corners. The truth is that one reason why we find the weather less pleasant, and the flowers fewer than our forefathers did, is that we keep May-day eleven days earlier in the year than they used to do.

To explain how this is, I must try and explain what Old Style and New Style—in reckoning the days of the year—mean.

First let me ask you how you can count the days. Supposing

you wish to remain just one day and night in a certain place, how will you know when you have stayed the proper time? In one of two ways. Either you will count twenty-four hours on the clock, or you will stay through all the light of one day, and all the darkness of one night. That is, you will count time either by the Clock or by the Sun.

Now we say that there are 365 days in the year. But there are really a few odd hours and minutes and seconds into the bargain. The reason of this is that the Sun does not go by the Clock in making the days and nights. Sometimes he spends rather more than twenty-four hours by the Clock over a day and night; sometimes he takes less. On the whole, during the year, he uses up more time than the Clock does.

The Clock makes exactly 365 days of 24 hours each. The Sun makes 365 days, 5 hours, 48 minutes, 49 seconds, and a tiny bit besides.

Now in time these odd hours added together would come to days, and the days to years. About fifteen hundred years of this little difference between the Sun and the Clock would bring it up to a year. So that if you went by the Clock you would say, "It is fifteen hundred years since such a thing happened." And if you went by the Sun you would say, "It is fifteen hundred and one years since it happened."

Men who could think and calculate saw how inconvenient this would be, and what mistakes it would lead to. If the difference did not come to much in their lifetime, they could see that it would come to a serious error for other people some day. So Julius Caesar thought he would pull the Clock and the Sun together by adding one day every four years to the Clock's year to make up for the odd hours the Sun had been spinning out during the three years before. The odd day was added to the month of February, and that year (in which there are three hundred and sixty-six days) is called Leap Year.

You remember the old saw—

"Thirty days hath September,
April, June, and November;
February hath twenty-eight alone,
All the rest have thirty-one;
Except in Leap Year, at which time
February's days are twenty-nine."

This is called the Old Style of reckoning.

Now I dare say you think the matter was quite settled; but it was not, unfortunately—the odd day every four years was just a tiny little bit too much, and now the Clock was spending more time over her years than the Sun. After more than sixteen hundred years the small mistake was becoming serious, and Pope Gregory XIII decided that we must not have so many leap years. For the future, in every four hundred years, three of the Clock's extra days must be given up, and ten days were to be left out of count at once to make up for the mistakes of years past.

This change is what is called the New Style of Reckoning. Pope Gregory began it in the year 1582, but we did not adopt it in England till 1752, and as we had then nearly two hundred years more of the little mistake to correct, *we* had to leave *eleven* days out of count. In Russia, where our new Princess comes from, they have not got it yet. The New Style was begun in England on September the 2nd. The next day, instead of being called September the 3rd, was called September the 14th. Since then we have gone on quite steadily, and played no more tricks with either the Sun's year or the Clock's year.

I wonder what happened in the year 1752 to all the children whose birthdays came between September the 2nd and September the 14th! I hope their birthday presents did not drop through because his Majesty George the Second had let eleven birthdays slip out of that year's calendar, to get the Clock and the Sun to work comfortably together.

Now I think you will be able to see that in the next year after this change, May-day was kept eleven days earlier in the Sun's year than the year before; and it has been at an earlier season ever since, and therefore in colder weather. May-day in the Old Style would have come this year about the middle of the month; and as years rolled on it would have been kept later and later in the summer, and thus in warmer and warmer weather, because of that little mistake of Julius Caesar. At last, instead of complaining that the May is not out by May-day, people would have had to complain that it was over.

Now in the New Style we keep May-day almost in Spring, and, thanks to Pope Gregory's clever arrangement, we shall always keep it at the same season.

It is not always cold on a May-day even in the north of England. I have a vivid remembrance of at least one which was most balmy; and, when they are warm enough for out-door enjoyment, the early days of the year seem, like the early hours of the day, to have an exquisite freshness peculiarly their own. Then the month of May, as a whole, is certainly the month of flowers in the woods and fields. Autumn is the gayest season of the garden, but Spring and early Summer give us the prettiest of the wild-flowers.

"Among the changing months May stands confest
The sweetest, and in fairest colours drest."

That fine weather is not quite to be relied upon for May-day, even in the Old Style, some of the old May-day customs seem to suggest. In the Isle of Man it was the custom not only to have a "Queen of May," but also a "Queen of Winter." The May Queen was, as elsewhere, some pretty and popular damsel, gaily dressed, and with a retinue of maids of honour. The Winter Queen was a man or boy dressed in woman's clothes of the warmest kind—"woollen hood, fur tippet," &c. Fiddles and flutes were played before the May Queen and her followers, whilst the Queen of Winter and her troop marched to the sound of the tongs and cleaver. The rival companies met on a common and had a mock battle, symbolizing the struggle of Winter and Summer for supremacy. If the Queen of Winter's forces contrived to capture the Queen of May, her floral majesty had to be ransomed by payment of the expenses of the day's festivity.

Whether the Queen of Winter conquered in bad weather, and her fairer rival when the season was warm and the flowers abundant, we are not told.

This ceremony was probably learnt from the Danes and Norwegians, who were long masters of the Isle of Man. *Olaus Magnus*, speaking of the May-day customs of the Goths and Southern Swedes, says, "The captain of one band hath the name and appearance of Winter, is clothed in skins of beasts, and he and his band armed with fire-forks. They fling about ashes, by way of prolonging the reign of Winter; while another band, whose captain is called Florro, represents Spring, with green boughs such as the season affords. These parties skirmish in sport, and the mimic contest concludes with a general feast."

A few years ago in the Isle of Man the hillsides blazed with bonfires and resounded to horns on the 11th of May (May-eve, Old Style). "May flowers" were put at the doors of houses and cattle-sheds, and these were not hawthorn blossoms, but the flowers of the kingcup, or marsh marigold. Crosses made of sprays of mountain ash were worn the same night, and they, the bonfires and May flowers, were reckoned charms against "wizards, witches, enchanters, and mountain hags."

At Helston, in Cornwall, May-day seems to have been known by the name of Furry Day. Perhaps a corruption of "Flora's Day." People wore hawthorn in their hats, and danced hand-in-hand through the town to the sound of a fiddle. This particular performance was known as a "faddy."

It is probable that some of our May-day customs came from the Romans, who kept the festival of Flora, the goddess of flowers, at this season. Others, perhaps, have a different, if not an older source. One custom was certainly common to both nations. When the feast of Flora was celebrated, the young Romans went into the woods and brought back green boughs with which they decked the houses.

To "go a-Maying" is in fact the principal ceremony of the day wherever kept, and for whatever reason. In the north of England children and young folk "were wont to rise a little after midnight on the morning of May-day, and walk to some neighbouring wood accompanied with music and the blowing of horns, where they broke down branches from the trees, and adorned them with nosegays and crowns of flowers. This done, they returned homewards with their booty about the time of sunrise, and made their doors and windows triumph in the flowery spoil." Stubbs, in the *Anatomie of Abuses* (A.D. 1585), speaks of this custom as common to "every parish, town, and village." The churches, as well as the houses, seem in some places to have been dressed with flowers and greenery.

In an old MS. of the sixteenth century it is said that on the feast of SS. Philip and James, the Eton boys were allowed to go out at four o'clock in the morning to gather May to dress their rooms, and sweet herbs to perfume them, "if they can do it without wetting their feet!"

Thirty or forty years ago May-day decorations, in some country places, consisted of strewing the cottage doorsteps with daisies, or other flowers.

In Hertfordshire a curious custom obtained of decking the neighbours' doors with May if they were popular, and with nettles if they were the reverse.

In Lancashire rustic wags put boughs of various trees at the doors of the girls of the neighbourhood. Each tree had a meaning (well known in the district), sometimes complimentary, and sometimes the reverse.

In France it was customary for lovers to deck over-night the houses of the ladies they wished to please, and school-boys paid a like compliment to their masters. They do not seem, however, to have been satisfied with nosegays or even with green branches; they transplanted young trees from the woods to the side of the door they wished to honour, and then decked them with ribbons, &c. There is a curious record that "Henry II., wishing to recompense the clerks of Bazoche for their good services in quelling an insurrection in Guienne, offered them money; but they would only accept the permission granted them by the king, of cutting in the royal woods such trees as they might choose for the planting of the May—a privilege which existed at the commencement of the French Revolution." In Cornwall, too, it seems to have been the custom to plant "stumps of trees" before the houses, as well as to decorate them with boughs and blossoms. And Mr. Aubrey (1686) says, "At Woodstock in Oxon they every

May-eve goe into the parke, and fetch away a number of haw-thorne-trees, which they set before their dores; 'tis a pity that they make such a destruction of so fine a tree."

One certainly agrees with Mr. Aubrey. Thorns are slow to grow, hard to transplant, and very lovely when they are old. It is not to be regretted that such ruthless destruction of them has gone out of fashion.

In Ireland "tall slender trees" seem to have been set up before the doors, as well as "a green bush, strewed over with yellow flowers, which the meadows yield plentifully." A writer, speaking of this in 1682, adds, "A stranger would go nigh to imagine that they were all signs of ale-sellers, and that all houses were ale-houses," referring to the old custom of a bunch of green as the sign of an inn, which is illustrated by the proverb, "Good wine needs no bush." I have an old etching of a river-side inn, in which the sign is a garland hanging on a pole.

I fancy the yellow flowers must have been cowslips, which the green fields of Erin do indeed "yield plentifully."

Besides these private May-trees, every village had its common Maypole, gaily adorned with wreaths and flags and ribbons, and sometimes painted in spiral lines of colour. The Welsh Maypoles seem to have been made from birch-trees, elms were used in Cornwall, and young oaks in other parts of England. Round these Maypoles the young villagers danced, and green booths were often set up on the grass near them.

In many villages the Maypole was as much a fixture as the parish stocks, but when a new one was required, it was brought home on May-eve in grand procession with songs and instrumental music. I am afraid there is a good deal of evidence to show that the Maypoles were not always honestly come by! However, the Puritan writers (from whose bitter and detailed complaints we learn most of what we know about the early English May-day customs) are certainly prejudiced, and perhaps not quite trustworthy witnesses. One good man groans lamentably: "What adoe make our young men at the time of May? Do they not use night watchings to rob and steale young trees out of other men's grounde, and bring them into their parishe, with minstrels playing before?"

But as the theft must have been committed with all the publicity that a fixed day, a large crowd, and a full band could ensure, and as we seem to have no record of interference at the time, or prosecutions afterwards, I hope we may infer that the owners of the woods did not grudge one tree for the village Maypole. A quainter vengeance seems to have sometimes followed the trespass. Honesty was at a discount. What had been once stolen was liable to be re-stolen. There seems to have been great rivalry among the villages as to which had the best Maypole. The happy parish which could boast the finest was not left at ease in its supremacy, for the lads of the other villages were always on the watch to steal it. A record of this custom amongst the Welsh reminds one that Wales was at once the land of bards and the home of Taffy the Thief. "If successful," says Owen, speaking of these Maypole robbers, they "had their feats recorded in songs."

In old times oxen were commonly used for farmwork, and it seems that they had their share in the May fun. Another Puritan writer says, "They have twentie or fortie yoke of oxen, every oxe having a sweete nosegaie of flowers tyed on the tippe of his hornes, and these oxen draw home this Maie poole."

How well one can imagine their slow swinging pace,

unmoved by the shouts and music which would stir a horse's more delicate nerves! Their broad moist noses; their large, liquid eyes, and, doubtless, a certain sense of pride in their "sweet nosegaies," like the pride of the Beast of a Regiment in his badge.

Horses, too, came in for their share of May decorations. It was an old custom to give the waggoner a ribbon for his team at every inn he passed on May-day.

In the last century there was a fixed Maypole near Horncastle, in Lincolnshire, to which the boys made a pilgrimage in procession every May-day with May-gads in their hands. May-gads are white willow wands, peeled, and dressed with cowslips.

There was a fixed Maypole in the Strand for many years—or rather a succession of Maypoles. One, when only four years old, was given to Sir Isaac Newton to make a stand for his telescope, and another seems to have had a narrow escape from being handed over to a less celebrated astronomer, some years later.

The wandering Maypole, with its Queen of the May and her chimney-sweeps, is a modern compound of the village Maypole and May Queen with the May games in which (as in the Christmas festivities) morris-dancers played a part. The May-day morris-dancers, like the Christmas mummers, performed sword-dances and sang appropriate doggerels in costume. The characters represented at one time or another were Maid Marian or the May Queen, Robin Hood or Lord of the May, Friar Tuck, Will Scarlet, Little John Stokesley, Tom the Piper, Mad Moll and her Husband, Mutch, the Fool and the Hobby Horse. Archery was amongst the May-day sports, especially in the company of Robin Hood. The Summer King and Queen were perhaps the oldest characters.

They seem to be identical with the Lord and Lady, and sometimes to have been merged in Robin Hood and Maid Marian.

"Maid Marian fair as ivory bone,
Scarlet, and Mutch, and Little John."

The King and Queen of May are spoken of in the thirteenth century, but morris-dancing at May-time does not seem to date earlier than Henry VII., and is not so old a custom as the immemorial one of going a-Maying

"To bring the summer home
The summer and the May-O!"

This was not confined to young people or to country-folk. Chaucer says that on May-day early "fourth goth al the court, both most and lest, to fetche the flowres fresh, and braunch, and blome," and Henry VIII. kept May-day very orthodoxly in the early years of his reign.

Milkmaids have been connected with May-day customs from an early period. Perhaps because syllabub and cream were the recognized dainties of the festival. In Northumberland a ring used to be dropped into the syllabub and fished for with a ladle. Whoever got it was to be the first married of the party. An odd old custom in Suffolk suggests that the hawthorn was not always ready even for the Old Style May-day. Any farm-servant who could find a branch in full blossom might claim a dish of cream for breakfast. The milkmaids who supplied London and other places used to dress themselves gaily on May-day and go round from house to house performing a dance, and receiving gratuities from their customers. On their heads—instead of a milk-pail— they carried a curious trophy, called the "Milkmaids' Garland," made of silver or pewter jugs, cups, and other pieces of plate, which they borrowed for the occasion, and which shone out of a mass of greenery and flowers. Possibly these were at first the pewter measures with which they served out the milk. The music to which the milkmaids' dance was performed, was the jangling of bells of different tones depending from a round plate of brass mounted upon a Maydecked pole; but a bag-pipe or fiddle was sometimes substituted.

Cream, syllabub, and dainties compounded with milk, belong in England to the May festival. In Germany there is a "May drink" (said to be very nice) made by putting woodruff into white Rhine wine, in the proportion of a handful to a quart. Black currant, balm, or peppermint leaves are sometimes added, and water and sugar.

The milkmaids' place has been completely usurped by the sweeps, who clatter a shovel and broom instead of the old plate and bells, and who seem to have added the popular Jack-in-the-green to the entertainment. Jack-in-the-green's costume is very simple. A wicker-work frame of an extinguisher shape, thickly covered with green, is supported by the man who carries it, and who peeps through a hole left for the purpose. May-day has become the Sweeps' Carnival. Mrs. Montague (whose son is said to have been stolen for a sweep in his childhood, and afterwards found) used to give the sweeps of London a good dinner every May-day, on the lawn before her house in Portman Square.

Another May-day custom is that of the choristers assembling at five o'clock in the morning on the top of the beautiful tower of Magdalen College, Oxford, and ushering in the day with singing. At the same time boys of the city armed with tin trumpets, called "May-horns," assemble beneath the tower, and contribute more sound than harmony to the celebration. Let us hope that it is not strictly a part of the old ceremony, but rather a minor manifestation of "Town and Gown" feeling, that the town boys jeer the choristers, and in return are pelted with rotten eggs. The origin of this special Oxford custom is said to be a requiem which was sung on the tower for the soul of Henry VII., founder of the College. In the villages girls used to carry round May-garlands. The party consisted of four children. Two girls in white dresses and gay ribbons carried the garland, and were followed by a boy and girl called "Lord and Lady," linked together by a white handkerchief, of which each held an end. The Lady carried the purse, and when she received a donation the Lord doffed his cap and kissed her. They sang a doggerel rhyme, and the form in which money was asked was, "Please to handsel the Lord and Lady's purse."

One cannot help thinking that some of our flowers, such as Milkmaids, Lords and Ladies, and Jack-in-the-green Primrose, bear traces of having got their common names at the great flower festival of the year.

In Cornwall boys carried the May-garland, which was adorned with painted birds' eggs. Old custom gave these young rogues the privilege of drenching with water from a bucket any one whom they caught abroad on May-morning without a sprig of May.

Mr. Aubrey says (1686): "At Oxford, the boyes do blow cows' horns all night; and on May-day the young maids of every parish carry about their parish garlands of flowers, which afterwards they hang up in their churches."

A generation or more ago the little boys of Oxford used to blow horns early on May-day—as they said—"to call up the old maids." There was once a custom in Lynn for the workhouse children to be allowed to go out with horns and garlands every May-day, after which a certain worthy gentleman gave them a good dinner.

In Cambridgeshire, within the present century, the children had a doll dressed as the "May Lady," before which they set a table with wine and food on it; they also begged money and garlands for "the poor May Lady."

There are some quaint superstitions connected with May-day and May-blossom. To bathe the face in the dew of a May morning was reckoned an infallible recipe for a good complexion. A bath of May dew was also supposed to strengthen weakly children. Girls divined for dreams of their future husbands with a sprig of hawthorn gathered before dusk on May-eve, and carried home in the mouth without speaking. Hawthorn rods were used at all seasons of the year to divine for water and minerals. Bunches of May fastened against houses were supposed to keep away witches and venomous reptiles, and to bring prosperity in various shapes.

The Irish of the neighbourhood of Killarney have a pretty superstition that on May-day the O'Donoghue, a popular prince of by-gone days, returns from the land of Immortal Youth beneath the water to bless the country over which he once ruled.

Some curious customs among the Scotch Highlanders (who call May 1st *Beltan* Day) have nothing in common with our Green Festival except as celebrating the Spring. They seem to be the remains of very ancient heathen sacrifices to Baal. They were performed by the herdsmen of the district, and included an open-air feast of cakes and custard, to which every one contributed, and which was cooked upon a fire on a turf left in the centre of a square trench which had been dug for the purpose. Some custard was poured out by way of libation. Every one then took a cake of oatmeal, on which nine knobs had been pinched up before baking, and turning his face to the fire threw the knobs over his shoulder, some as offerings to the supposed guardians of the flock, and the rest in propitiation of beasts and birds of prey, with the form "This to thee, O Fox! spare my lambs! This to thee, O hooded Crow!" &c. In some places the boys of the hamlet met on the moors for a similar feast, but the turf table was round, and the oatcake divided into bits, one of which was blackened with charcoal. These being drawn from a bonnet, the holder of the black bit was held *devoted* to Baal, and had to leap three times over the bonfire.

I do not know of any children's games that were peculiar to May-day. In France they had a May-day game called *Sans-vert*. Those who played had to wear leaves of the hornbeam-tree, and these were to be kept fresh, under penalty of a fine. The chief object of the players was to surprise each other without the proper leaves, or with faded specimens.

A stupid old English custom of making fools of your friends on the 1st of May as well as on the 1st of April hardly deserves the title of a game. The victims were called "May goslings."

One certainly would not expect to meet with anything like "Aunt Sally" among May-day games, especially with the "May Lady" for butt! But not the least curious part of a very curious account of May-day in Huntingdonshire, which was sent to *Notes and Queries* some years ago, is the pelting of the May Lady as a final ceremony of the festival. The May-garlands carried round in Huntingdonshire villages appear to have been more like the "milkmaids' garland" than genuine wreaths. They were four to five feet high, extinguisher-shaped, with every kind of spring flower in the apex, and with ribbons and gay kerchiefs hanging down from the base, by the round rim of which the garland was carried; the flower-peak towering above, and the gay streamers depending below. Against this erection (not unlike the "mistletoe boughs" of the North of England) was fastened a gaily-dressed doll. The bearers were two little girls, who acted as maids of honour to the May Queen. Mr. Cuthbert Bede describes her Majesty as he saw her twenty years ago. She wore a white frock, and a bonnet with a white veil. A wreath of real flowers lay on the bonnet. She carried a pocket-handkerchief bag and a parasol (the latter being regarded as a special mark of dignity). An "Odd Fellows'" ribbon and badge completed her costume. The maids of honour bore the garland after her, whose peak was crowned with "tulips, anemones, cowslips, kingcups, meadow-orchis, wall-flower, primrose, crown-imperial, lilac, laburnum," and "other bright flowers." Votive offerings were dropped into the pocket-handkerchief bag, and with these a feast was provided for the children. If the gifts had been liberal, "goodies" were proportionately plentiful. Finally, the May-garland was suspended from a rope hung across the village street, and the children pelted the May-doll with balls provided for the occasion. Their chief aim was to hit her nose.

Another correspondent of *Notes and Queries* speaks of ropes with dolls suspended from them as being stretched across every village street in Huntingdonshire on May-day, and adds, that not only ribbons and flowers were attached to these swinging May Ladies, but articles of every description, including "candlesticks, snuffers, spoons, and forks."

There are no May carols rivalling those of Christmas, and the verses which children sing with their garlands are very bald as a rule.

A Maypole song of the Gloucestershire children would do very well to dance to—

"Round the Maypole, trit-trit-trot!

See what a Maypole we have got;
Fine and gay,
Trip away,
Happy is our New May-day."

I have read of a pretty old Italian custom for the friends of prisoners to assemble outside the prison walls on May-day and join with them in songs. They are also said to have permission to have a May-day feast with them.

Under all its various shapes, and however adapted to the service of particular heathen deities, or to very rude social festivity, the root of the May-day festival lies in the expression of feelings both natural and right. Thankfulness for the return of Spring, anxiety for the coming harvests of the fruits of the earth, and that sense of exhilaration and hopefulness which the most exquisite of seasons naturally brings—brings more strongly perhaps in the youth of a nation, in those earlier stages of civilization when men are very dependent upon the weather, and upon the produce of their own particular neighbourhood—brings most strongly of all to one's own youth, to the light heart, the industrious fancy, the uncorrupted taste of childhood.

May-day seems to me so essentially a children's festival, that I think it is a great pity that English children should allow it to fall into disuse. One certainly does not love flowers less as one grows up, but they are more like persons, and their ways are more mysterious to one in childhood. The cares of grown-up life, too, are not of the kind from which we can easily get a whole holiday. We should do well to try oftener than we do. Wreaths do not become us, and we have allowed our joints to grow too stiff for Maypole dancing. But we who used to sigh for whole holidays can give them! We can prepare the cakes and cream, and provide ribbons for the Maypole, and show how garlands were made in our young days. We are very grateful for wild-flowers for the drawing-room. To say the truth, they last longer with us than with the children, and perhaps we combine the delicate hues of spring, and lighten our nosegays by grass and sword-flags and rushes with more cunning fingers than those of the little ones who gathered them.

For these is reserved the real bloom of May-day! And the orthodox customs are so various, that families of any size or age may pick and choose. One brother and sister can be Lord and Lady of the May. One sister among many brothers must be May Queen without opposition. Those of the party most apt to catch cold in the treacherous sunshine and damp winds of spring should certainly represent the Winter Queen and her attendants, in the warmest possible clothing and the thickest of boots. The morning air will then probably only do them a great deal of good. It is not desirable to dig up the hawthorn-trees, or to try to do so, even with wooden spades. The votive offering of flowers for her drawing-room should undoubtedly await Mamma when she comes down to breakfast, and I heartily wish her as abundant a variety as Mr. Cuthbert Bede saw on the Huntingdonshire garland. That Nurse should have a bunch of May is only her due; and of course the nursery must be decorated. Long strips of coloured calico form good ribbons for the Maypole. Bows and arrows are easily made. It is also easy to cut one's fingers in notching the arrows. When you are tired of dancing, you can be Robin Hood's merry men, and shoot. When all the arrows are lost, and you have begun to quarrel about the target, it will be well to hang up an old doll and throw balls at her nose. Dressing-up is, at any time, a delightful amuse-ment, and there is a large choice among May-day characters. No wardrobe can fail to provide the perfectly optional costumes of Mad Moll and her husband. There are generally some children who never will learn their parts, and who go astray from every pre-arranged plan. By any two such the last-named characters should be represented. In these, as in all children's games, "the more the merrier"; and as there is no limit to the number of sweeps, the largest of families may revel in burnt cork, even if dust-pans in proportion fail. If a bonfire is more appropriate to the weather than a Maypole, we have the comfort of feeling that it is equally correct.

It is hardly needful to impress upon the boys what vigour the blowing of horns and penny trumpets will impart to the ceremonies; but they may require to be reminded that Eton men in old days were only allowed to go a-Maying on condition that they did not wet their feet!

Above all, out-door May Fun is no fun unless the weather is fine; and I hope this little paper will show that if the 1st of May is chilly, and the flowers are backward, nothing can be more proper than to keep our feast on the 12th of May— *May-day, Old Style*. If the Clerk of the Weather Office is unkind on both these days, give up out-door fun at once, and prepare for a fancy-ball in the nursery; all the guests to be dressed as May-day characters. Garland-making and country expeditions can then be deferred till Midsummer-day. It is not *very* long to wait, and penny trumpets do not spoil with keeping.

But do not be defrauded of at least one early ramble in the woods and fields. It is well, in the impressionable season of life, to realize, if only occasionally, how much of the sweetest air, the brightest and best hours of the day, people spend in bed. Any one who goes out every day before breakfast knows how very seldom he is kept in by bad weather. For one day when it rains very early there are three or four when it rains later. But we wait till the world has got dirty, and the air full of the smoke of thousands of break-fasts, and clouds are beginning to gather, and then we say England has a horrible climate. I do not believe in many quack medical prescriptions, but I have the firmest faith in May dew as a wash for the complexion. Any morning dew is nearly as efficacious if it is gathered in warm clothes, thick boots, and at a sufficient distance from home.

There are some households in which there are no children, and there are some in which the good things of this life are very abundant. To these it may not be very impertinent to suggest a remembrance of the old alderman of Lynn's kindly benefaction. To beg leave for the children of the workhouse to gather May-day nosegays for you, and to give them a May feast afterwards, would be to give pleasure of a kind in which such unhomely lives are most deficient. A country ramble "with an object," and the grace-in-memory of a traditionary holiday and feast, shared in common with many homes and with other children.

To go a-Maying "to fetche the flowres fresh" is indeed the best part of the whole affair.

But, when the sunny bank under the hedge is pale with primroses, when dog-violets spread a mauve carpet over clearings in the little wood, if cowslips be plentiful though oxslips are few, and rare orchids bless the bogs of our locality, pushing strange insect heads, through beds of *Drosera* bathed in perpetual dew—then, dear children, restrain the natural impulse to grub everything up and take the whole flora of the neighbourhood home in your pinafores. In the first place, you can't. In the second place, it would be very hard on other people if you could. Cull skilfully, tenderly, unselfishly, and remember what my mother used to say to me and my brothers and sisters when we were "collecting" anything, from fresh-water algae to violet roots for our very own gardens, "*Leave some for the Naiads and Dryads.*"

IN MEMORIUM, MARGARET GATTY

In Memoriam.

MARGARET,

[Daughter of the Rev. Alexander John Scott, D.D.]

(LORD NELSON'S CHAPLAIN, AND THE FRIEND IN WHOSE ARMS HE DIED AT TRAFALGAR),

was Born June 3rd, 1809.

In 1839 she was Married to the Rev. Alfred Gatty,

OF ECCLESFIELD, YORKSHIRE,

where she Died on October the 4th, 1873, aged 64.

My mother became editor of *Aunt Judy's Magazine* in May 1866. It was named after one of her most popular books— *Aunt Judy's Tales*; and Aunt Judy became a name for herself with her numerous child-correspondents.

The ordinary work of editorship was heavily increased by her kindness to tyro authors, and to children in want of everything, from advice on a life-vocation to old foreign postage stamps. No consideration of the value of her own time could induce her to deal summarily with what one may call her magazine children, and her correspondents were of all ages and acquirements, from nursery aspirants barely beyond pothooks to such writers as the author of *A Family Man for Six Days*, and other charming Australian reminiscences, who still calls her his "literary godmother."

The peculiar relation in which she stood to so many of the readers of *Aunt Judy* has been urged upon me as a reason for telling them something more about her than that she is dead and gone, especially as by her peremptory wish no larger record of her life will ever be made public. I need hardly disclaim any thought of expressing an opinion on her natural powers, or the value of those labours from which she rests; but whatever of good there was in them she devoted with real affectionate interest to the service of a much larger circle of children than of those who now stand desolate before her empty chair. And those whom she has so long taught have, perhaps, some claim upon the lessons of her good example.

Most well-loved pursuits, perhaps most good habits of our lives, owe their origin to our being stirred at one time or another to the imitation of some one better, or better gifted than ourselves. We can remember dates at which we began to copy what our present friends may fancy to be innate peculiarities of our own character. The conviction of this truth, and of the strong influence which little details of lives we admire have in forming our characters in childhood, persuade me to the hard task of writing at all of my dear mother, and guide me in choosing those of the things that we remember about her which may help her magazine children on matters about which they have oftenest asked her counsel.

Many of her own innumerable hobbies had such origins, I know. The influence of German literature on some of her writings is very obvious, and this most favourite study sprang chiefly from a very early fit of hero-worship for Elizabeth Smith, whose precocious and unusual acquirements she was stirred to emulate, and whose enthusiasm for Klopstock she caught. The fly-leaf of her copy of the Smith *Remains* bears (in her handwriting) the date 1820, with her name as Meta Scott; a form of her own Christian name which she probably adopted in honour of Margaretta—or Meta—Klopstock, and by which she was well known to friends of her youth.

She often told us, too, of the origin of another of her accomplishments. She was an exquisite caligraphist. Not only did she write the most beautiful and legible of handwritings, but, long before illuminating was "fashionable," she illuminated on vellum; not by filling up printed texts or copying ornamental letters from handbooks of the art, but in valiant emulation of ancient MSS.; designing her own initial letters, with all varieties of characters, with "strawberry" borders, and gold raised and burnished as in the old models. I do not know when she first saw specimens of the old illuminations, for which she had always the deepest admiration, but it was in a Dante fever that she had resolved to write beautifully, because fine penmanship had been among the accomplishments of the great Italian poet. How well she succeeded her friends and her printers knew to their comfort! To Dante she dedicated some of her best efforts in this art. In 1826, when she was seventeen, she began to translate the *Inferno* into English verse. She made fair copies of each canto in exquisite writing, and dedicated them to various friends on covers which she illuminated. The most highly-finished was that dedicated to an old friend, Lord Tyrconnel, and the only plain one was the one dedicated to another friend, Sir Thomas Lawrence. The dedication was written in fine long characters, but there was no painting on the cover of the canto dedicated to the painter.

I do not know at what date my mother began to etch on copper. It was a very favourite pursuit through many years of her life, both before and after her marriage. She never sketched much in colour, but her pencil-drawings are amongst the most valuable legacies she has left us. Trees were her favourite subjects. One of her most beautiful drawings in my possession is of a tree, marked to fall, beneath which she wrote:

"Das ist das Loos des Schoenen auf der Erde."[2]

Of another talent nothing now remains to us but her old music-books and memories of long evenings when she played Weber and Mozart.

But to a large circle of friends, most of whom have gone before her, she was best known as a naturalist in the special department of phycology. She has left a fine collection of British and foreign sea-weeds and zoophytes. Never permitted the privilege of foreign travel—for which she so often longed—her sea-spoils have been gathered from all shores by those who loved her; and there are sea-weeds yet in press sent by *Aunt Judy* friends from Tasmania, which gave pleasure to the last days of her life. She did so keenly enjoy everything at which she worked that it is difficult to say in which of her hobbies she found most happiness; but I am disposed to give her natural history pursuits the palm.

Natural history brought her some of her dearest friends. Dr. Johnston, of Berwick-on-Tweed, to whom she dedicated the first volume of the *Parables from Nature*, was one of these; and with Dr. Harvey (author of the *Phycologia Britannica*, &c.) she corresponded for ten years before they met. Like herself, he combined a playful and poetical fancy with the scientific faculty, and they had sympathy together in the distinctive character of their religious belief, and in the worship of God in His works. But these, and many others, have "gone before."

One of her "collections" was an unusual one. Through nearly forty years she collected the mottoes on old sun-dials, and made sketches of the dials themselves. In this also she had many helpers, and the collection, which had swelled to about four hundred, was published last year. Amateur bookbinding and mowing were among the more eccentric of her hobbies. With the latter she infected Mr. Tennyson, and sent him a light Scotch scythe like her own.

The secret of her success and of her happiness in her labours was her thoroughness. It was a family joke that in the garden she was never satisfied to dabble in her flower-beds like other people, but would always clear out what she called "the Irish corners," and attack bits of waste or neglected ground from which everybody else shrank. And amongst our neighbours in the village, those with whom, day after day, time after time, she would plead "the Lord's controversy," were those with whom every one else had failed. Some old village would-be sceptic, half shame-faced, half conceited, who had not prayed for half a lifetime, or been inside a church except at funerals; careworn mothers fossilized in the long neglect, of religious duties; sinners whom every one else thought hopeless, and who most-of all counted themselves so—if God indeed permits us hereafter to bless those who led us to Him here, how many of these will rise up and call her blessed!

Her strong powers of sympathy were not confined to human beings alone. A more devoted lover of "beasts" can hardly exist. The household pets were about her to the end; and she only laughed when the dogs stole the bread and butter from her helpless hands.

Her long illness, perhaps, did less to teach us to do without her, than long illnesses commonly do; because her sick-room was so little like a sick-room, and her interests never narrowed to the fretful circle of mere invalid fears and fancies. The strong sense of humour, which never left her, helped her through many a petty annoyance; and to the last she kept one of her most striking qualities, so well described by Trench—

—"a child's pure delight in little things."

Whatever interest this little record of some of my mother's tastes and acquirements may have for her young readers, its value must be in her example.

Whatever genius she may have had, her industry was far more remarkable. The pen of a ready writer is not grasped by all fingers, and gifts are gifts, not earnings. But to cultivate the faculties God has given us to His glory, to lose petty cares, ignoble pleasures, and small grievances, in the joy of studying His great works, to be good to His creatures, to be truthful beyond fear or flattery, to be pure of heart and tongue far beyond the common, to keep up an honest, zealous war with wickedness, and never to lose heart or hope for wicked men—these things are within the power as well as the ambition of us all.

I must point out to some of the young aspirants after her literary fame, that though the date in Elizabeth Smith's *Remains* shows my mother to have been only eleven years old when she got it, and though she worked and studied indefatigably all her girlhood, her first original work was not published till she was forty-two years old.

Of the lessons of her long years of suffering I cannot speak. A form of paralysis which left her brain as vigorous as ever, stole the cunning from her hand, and the use of her limbs and voice, through ten years of pain and privation, in which she made a willing sacrifice of her powers to the will of God.

If some of her magazine children who enjoy "advantages" she never had, who visit places and see sights for which she longed in vain, and who are spared the cross she bore so patiently, are helped by this short record of their old friend, it may somewhat repay the pain it has cost in writing.

Trench's fine sonnet was a great favourite of my mother's—

"To leave unseen so many a glorious sight,
To leave so many lands unvisited,
To leave so many books unread,
Unrealized so many visions bright;—
Oh! wretched yet inevitable spite
Of our short span, and we must yield our breath,
And wrap us in the unfeeling coil of death,
So much remaining of unproved delight,
But hush, my soul, and vain regrets be still'd;
Find rest in Him Who is the complement
Of whatsoe'er transcends our mortal doom,
Of broken hope and frustrated intent;
In the clear vision and aspect of Whom
All wishes and all longings are fulfill'd."

FOOTNOTES:

[Footnote 2: "Such is the lost of the beautiful upon earth."— *Wallenstein's Tod*.]

TALES OF THE KHOJA[3]

(Adapted from the Turkish.)

INTRODUCTION

"O my children!" said the story-teller, "do you indeed desire amusement by the words of my lips? Then shut your mouths, that the noise you make may be abated, and I may hear myself speak; and open your ears, that you may be entertained by the tales that I shall tell you. Shut your mouths and open your ears, I say, and you will, without doubt, receive pleasure from what I shall have to relate of Khoja Nasr-ed-Deen-Effendi.

"This Khoja was not altogether a wise man, nor precisely a fool, nor entirely a knave."

"It is true, O children, that his wisdom was flecked with folly, but what saith the proverb? 'No one so wise but he has some folly to spare.' Moreover, in his foolishness there was often a hidden meaning, as a letter is hid in a basket of dates—not for every eye.

"As to his knaveries, they were few, and more humorous than injurious. Though be it far from me, O children, as a man of years and probity, to defend the conduct of the Khoja to the Jew money-lender.

"What about the Jew money-lender, do you ask?"

"This is the tale."

Tale 1.—The Khoja and the Nine Hundred and Ninety-nine Pieces of Gold.

This Khoja was very poor.

One day, wishing for a piece of gold, he corrected himself, saying: "It costs no more to wish for a thousand pieces than for one. I wish for a thousand gold pieces."

And he repeated aloud—"I wish for a thousand pieces of gold. *I would not accept one less.*"

Now it so happened that he was overheard by a certain covetous Jew money-lender. This man was of a malicious disposition; and the poverty of the Khoja was a satisfaction to him. When he heard what the Khoja said he chuckled to himself, saying, "Truly this Khoja is a funny fellow, and it would be a droll thing to see him refuse nine hundred and ninety-nine pieces of gold. For without doubt he would keep his word."

And as he spoke, the Jew put nine hundred and ninety-nine gold pieces into a purse, and dropped the purse down the Khoja's chimney, with the intention of giving him annoyance.

The Khoja picked up the purse and opened it.

"Allah be praised!" he cried, "for the fulfilment of my desires. Here are the thousand pieces."

Meanwhile the Jew was listening at the chimney-top, and he heard the Khoja begin to count the coins. When he got to the nine hundred and ninety-ninth, and had satisfied himself that there was not another, he paused, and the Jew merchant held his breath.

At last the Khoja spoke.

"O my soul!" said he, "is it decent to spit in the face of good fortune for the sake of one gold piece in a thousand? Without doubt it is an oversight, and he who sent these will send the missing one also." Saying which, the Khoja put the money into his sash and sat down to smoke.

The Jew now became fidgety, and he hastened down to the Khoja's door, at which he knocked, and entering, said, "Good-day, Khoja Effendi. May I ask you to be good enough to restore to me my nine hundred and ninety-nine gold pieces?"

"Are you mad, O Jew money-lender?" replied the Khoja. "Is it likely that you would throw gold down my chimney? These pieces fell from heaven in fulfilment of my lawful desires."

"O my soul, Khoja!" cried the Jew, "I did it, indeed! It was a jest, O Khoja! You said, 'I will not take one less than a thousand,' wherefore I put nine hundred and ninety-nine pieces in the purse, and it was for a joke."

"I do not see the joke," said the Khoja, "but I have accepted the gold pieces." And he went on smoking.

The Jew money-lender now became desperate.

"Let us go to the magistrate," he cried. "The Cadi Effendi

shall decide between us."

"It is well said," replied the Khoja. "But it would not beseem a Khoja like myself to go through the public streets to the court on foot; and I am poor, and have no mule."

"O my soul!" said the Jew, "let not that trouble you. I will send and fetch one of my mules."

But when the mule was at the door, the Khoja said: "Is it fitting, O money-lender, that a Khoja like myself should appear in these rags before a Cadi Effendi? But I am poor, and have no suitable dress."

"Let not that be a hindrance, O Khoja!" said the Jew. "For I have a pelisse made of the most beautiful fur, which I will send for without delay."

In due time this arrived, and, richly clothed, the Khoja rode through the streets with a serene countenance, the Jew money-lender running after him in the greatest anxiety.

When they came before the Cadi, the Jew prostrated himself, and cried in piteous tones, "Help, O most noble Dispenser of Justice! This Khoja has stolen from me nine hundred and ninety-nine pieces of gold—and now he denies it."

Then the Cadi turned to the Khoja, who said: "O Cadi Effendi, I did indeed earnestly desire a thousand pieces of gold, and this purse came to me in fulfilment of my wishes. But when I counted the pieces I found one short. Then I said, 'The bountiful giver of these will certainly send the other also.' So I accepted what was given to me. But in this Jew money-lender is the spirit of covetousness. For half a farthing, O Cadi, he would, without doubt, lay claim to the beast I ride, or to the coat on my back."

"O my soul!" screamed the Jew. "It is indeed true that they are mine. The mule and the fur pelisse belong to me, O Cadi!"

"O you covetous rascal!" said the Cadi, "you will lay claim to my turban next, or to the Sultan's horses." And he commanded the Jew to be driven from his presence.

But the Khoja rode home again, and—he accepted the mule and the fur pelisse, as well as the nine hundred and ninety-nine pieces of gold.

Tale 2.—The Khoja at the Marriage Feast.

On the following day Khoja Effendi went to a marriage feast, dressed in his old clothes.

His appearance was indeed very shabby, and the attendants were almost disposed to refuse him admission, but he slipped in whilst honours and compliments were being paid on the arrival of some grander guests. Even those who knew him well were so much ashamed of his dress as to be glad to look another way to avoid saluting him.

All this was quickly observed by the Khoja, and after a few moments (during which no one asked him to be seated) he slipped out and ran home, where he put on the splendid fur pelisse which he had accepted from the Jew money-lender, and so returned to the door of the house of feasting.

Seeing a guest so richly apparelled draw near, the servants ran out to meet him with all signs of respect, and the master of the feast came out also to meet him with other guests, saluting him and saying, "Welcome, O most learned Khoja!" And all who knew him saluted him in like manner, and secretly blessed themselves that his acquaintance did them credit.

But the Khoja looked neither to the right hand nor to the left, and he made no reply.

Then they led him to the upper end of the table, crying, "Please to be seated, Khoja Effendi!"

Whereupon the Khoja seated himself, but he did not speak, and the guests stood round him, waiting to hear what should fall from his lips.

And when the Khoja had been served with food, he took hold of the sleeve of his pelisse and pulled it towards the dish, saying, in a tone of respect, "O most worthy and honourable pelisse! be good enough to partake of this dish. In the name of the Prophet I beseech you do not refuse to taste what has been hospitably provided."

"What is this, Khoja?" cried the people, "and what do you mean by offering food to a fur pelisse that can neither hear nor eat?"

"O most courteous entertainers!" replied the Khoja, "since the pelisse has commanded such respect at your hands, is it not proper that it should also partake of the food?"

Tale 3.—The Khoja's Slippers.

One day, when the idle boys of the neighbourhood were gathered together and ready for mischief, they perceived the Khoja approaching.

"Here comes this mad Khoja!" they said. "Let us now persuade him to climb the largest of these mulberry-trees, and whilst he is climbing we will steal his slippers."

And when the Khoja drew near, they cried, "O Khoja, here is

indeed a tree which it is not possible to climb."

The Khoja looked at the mulberry-tree and said, "You are in error, my children, any one of you could climb that tree."

But they said, "We cannot."

Then said the Khoja, "I, who am an old man, could climb that mulberry-tree."

Then the boys cried, "O most illustrious Khoja! we beseech of you to climb the tree before our eyes, that we may believe what you say, and also be encouraged to try ourselves."

"I will climb it," said the Khoja. Thereupon he kicked off his slippers as the children had anticipated; and tucking his skirts into his girdle, he prepared to climb.

But whilst they were waiting to steal his slippers, the Khoja put them into his pocket.

"Effendi Khoja," said the children, "wherefore do you not leave your slippers on the ground? What will you do with slippers up in the mulberry-tree?"

"O my children!" said the Khoja dryly, "it is good to be provided against everything. I may come upon a road further up."

Tale 4.—The Khoja and the Three Wise Men.

In the days of Effendi Nasr-ed-Deen Khoja there appeared in the world three Sages, who excelled in every science and in all wisdom.

Now it came to pass that in their journeys these wise men

passed through the country of the Sultan Ala-ed-Deen, who desired to see them, and to make them partake of his hospitality.

And when the Sultan had seen and heard them, he said: "O Sages, there is indeed nothing wanting to you but that you should embrace the faith and become Turks, and remain in my kingdom. Wherefore I beseech of you to do this without further delay."

Then the wise men replied to the Padisha: "We will, if it please you, ask three questions of your learned men. One question shall be asked by each of us, and if they are able to answer these questions, we will embrace your faith, and remain with you as you desire. And if not, we will depart in peace, and prolong our journeys as heretofore."

Then the Padisha replied: "So be it." And he assembled the learned men and counsellors of his kingdom, and the Sages put questions to them, which they could not answer.

Then the Sultan Ala-ed-Deen was full of wrath, and he said, "Is this my kingdom, and am I the ruler of it; and is there not indeed one man of my subjects wise enough to answer the questions of these unbelieving Sages?"

And his servants replied: "There is indeed no one who could answer these questions, except it be Khoja Nasr-ed-Deen Effendi."

Then the Sultan commanded, and they despatched a Tatar in all haste to summon Nasr-ed-Deen Effendi to the presence of the Padisha.

When the messenger arrived, he told his errand to the Khoja, who at once rose up, saddled his donkey, took a stick in his

Juliana Horatia Ewing

hand, and mounted, saying to the Tatar, "Go before me!"

Thus they came to the palace, and the Khoja entered the presence of the Sultan, and gave the salaam and received it in return. Then he was shown where to sit, and being seated, and having made a prayer for the Padisha, "O most noble Sultan," said he, "wherefore have you brought me hither, and what is your will with me?"

Then the Sultan explained the circumstances of the case, and the Khoja cried, "What are the questions? Let me hear them."

Then the first wise man came forward and said: "*My* question, most worshipful Effendi, is this: Where is the middle of the world?"

The Khoja, without an instant's hesitation, pointed with his stick to a fore-hoof of his donkey.

"There," said he, "exactly where my donkey's foot is placed—there is the centre of the earth."

"How do you know that?" asked the Sage.

"If you do not believe me," replied the Khoja, "measure for yourself. If you find it wrong one way or the other, I will acknowledge my error."

The second Sage now came forward and said: "O Khoja Effendi, how many stars are there on the face of this sky?"

"The same number," replied the Khoja, "as there are hairs on my donkey."

"How do you know that?" asked the wise man.

"If you do not believe me," replied the Khoja, "count for yourself. If there is a hair too few or too many, I will acknowledge my error."

"O most learned Khoja!" said the wise man, "have you indeed counted the hairs on your donkey?"

"O most venerable Sage!" replied the Khoja, "have you indeed numbered the stars of the sky?"

But as the Khoja spoke the third wise man came forward and said: "Most worshipful Effendi! Be pleased now to hear my question, and if you can answer it, we will conform to the wishes of the Sultan. How many hairs are there in my beard?"

"As many," replied the Khoja, "as there are hairs in my donkey's tail."

"How do you know that?" asked the wise man.

"If you do not believe me, count for yourself," said the Khoja.

But the wise man replied: "It is for you to count, and to prove to me the truth of what you say."

"With all my heart," replied the Khoja. "And I will do it in a way that cannot possibly fail. I shall first pull out a hair from your beard, and then one from my donkey's tail, and then another from your beard, and so on. Thus at the end it will be seen whether the number of the hairs of each kind exactly correspond."

But the wise man did not wait for this method of proof to be enforced by the Sultan. He hastily announced himself as a

Juliana Horatia Ewing

convert to the Padisha's wishes. The other two Sages followed his example, and their wisdom was for many years the light of the court of the Sultan Ala-ed-Deen.

Moreover, they became disciples of the Khoja.

Tale 5.—The Khoja's Donkey.

One day there came a man to the house of the Khoja to ask him for the loan of his donkey.

"The donkey is not at home," replied the Khoja, who was unwilling to lend his beast.

At this moment the donkey brayed loudly from within.

"O Khoja Effendi!" cried the man, "what you say cannot be true, for I can hear your donkey quite distinctly as I stand here."

"What a strange man you must be," said the Effendi. "Is it possible that you believe a donkey rather than me, who am grey-haired and a Khoja?"

Tale 6.—The Khoja's Gown.

One day the Khoja's wife, having washed her husband's gown, hung it out in the garden to dry.

Now in the dusk of the evening the Khoja repaired to his garden, where he saw, as he believed, a thief standing with outstretched arms.

"O you rascal!" he cried, "is it you who steal my fruit? But you shall do so no more."

And having called to his wife for his bow and arrows, the Khoja took aim and pierced his gown through the middle. Then without waiting to see the result he hastened into his house, secured the door with much care, and retired to rest.

When morning dawned, the Khoja went out into the garden, where perceiving that what he had hit was his own gown, he seated himself and returned thanks to the All-merciful Disposer of Events.

"Truly," said he, "I have had a narrow escape. If I had been inside it, I should have been dead long before this!"

Tale 7.—The Khoja and the Fast of Ramadan.

In a certain year, when the holy month of the fast of Ramadan was approaching, Khoja Nasr-ed-Deen took counsel with himself and resolved not to observe it.

"Truly," said he, "there is no necessity that I should fast like the common people. I will rather provide myself with a vase into which I will drop a stone every day. When there are thirty pebbles in the vase, I shall know that Ramadan is over, and I shall then be able to keep the feast of Bairam at the proper season."

Accordingly, on the first day of the month the Khoja dropped a stone into the vase, and so he continued to do day by day.

Now the Khoja had a little daughter, and it came to pass that one day the child, having observed the pebbles in the vase, went out and gathered a handful and added them to the rest. But her father was not aware of it.

On the twenty-fifth day of Ramadan the Khoja met at the Bazaar with certain of his neighbours, who said to him, "Be good enough, most learned Khoja, to tell us what day of the month it is."

"Wait a bit, and I will see," replied the Khoja. Saying this, he ran to his house, emptied the vase, and began to count the stones. To his amazement he found that there were a hundred and twenty!

"If I say as much as this," thought the Khoja, "they will call me a fool. Even half would be more than could be believed."

So he went back to the Bazaar and said, "It is the full forty-fifth of the month, quite that."

"O Khoja!" the neighbours replied, "there are only thirty days in a complete month, and do you tell us to-day is the forty-fifth?"

"O neighbours!" answered the Khoja, "believe me, I speak with moderation. If you look into the vase, you will find that according to its account to-day is the one hundred and twentieth."

Tale 8.—The Khoja and the Thief.

One day a thief got into the Khoja's house, and the Khoja watched him.

The thief poked here, there, and everywhere, and after collecting all that he could carry, he put the load on his back and went off.

The Khoja then came out, and hastily gathering up the few things which were left of his property, he put them on his own back, and hurried after the thief.

At last he arrived before the door of the thief's house, at which he knocked.

"What do you want?" said the thief.

"Why, we are moving into this house, aren't we?" said the Khoja. "I've brought the rest of the things."

Tale 9.—The Bird of Prey and the Piece of Soap.

One day the Khoja went with his wife to wash clothes at the head of a spring.

They had placed the soap beside them on the ground, and were just about to begin, when a black bird of prey swooped suddenly down, and snatching up the soap, flew away with it, believing it to be some kind of food.

"Run, Khoja, run!" cried the distracted wife. "Make haste, I beseech you, and catch that thief of a bird. He has carried off my soap."

"O wife!" replied the Khoja, "let him alone. He wants it more than we do, poor fellow! Our clothes are not half so black as what he has got on."

Tale 10.—The Khoja and the Wolves.

"Wife!" said the Khoja one day, "how do you know when a man is dead?"

"When his hands and feet have become cold, Khoja," replied the good woman, "I know that it is all over then. The man is dead."

Some time afterwards the Khoja went to the mountain to cut

Juliana Horatia Ewing

wood. It was in the winter, and after he had worked for an hour or two his hands and feet became very cold.

"It is really a melancholy thing," said he; "but I fear that there can be no doubt that I am dead. If this is the case, however, I have no business to be on my feet, much less to be chopping firewood which I have not lived to require." So he went and lay down under a tree.

By and by came the wolves, and they fell upon the Khoja's donkey, and devoured it.

The Khoja watched them from the place where he was lying.

"Ah, you brutes!" said he, "it is lucky for you that you have found a donkey whose master is dead, and cannot interfere."

Tale 11.—A Penny a Head.

The Turks shave their heads and allow their beards to grow. Thus the Khoja went every week to the barber to have his head shaved, and when it was done, the barber held out the mirror to him, that, having looked at himself, he might place a penny fee on the mirror as the custom is.

Now as he grew old the Khoja became very bald.

One day when he was about to be shaved, passing his hand over his head, he perceived that the crown was completely bald. But he said nothing, and having paid his penny, took his departure as usual.

Next week Khoja Effendi went again to the barber's.

When his head had been shaved he looked in the mirror as before; but he put nothing on it.

As he rose to depart, the barber stopped him, saying, "Most worshipful Effendi, you have forgotten to pay."

"My head is now half bald," said the Khoja; "will not one penny do for two shavings?"

Tale 12.—The Khoja a Cadi.

The late Khoja Effendi when he filled the office of Cadi had some puzzling cases to decide.

One day two men came before him, and one of them said, "This fellow has bitten my ear, O Cadi!"

"No, no, most learned Cadi!" said the other; "that is not true. He bit his own ear, and now tries to lay the blame upon me."

"One cannot bite his own ear," said the first man; "wherefore the lies of this scoundrel are obvious."

"Begone, both of you," said the Khoja; "but come back tomorrow, when I will give judgment."

When the men had gone, the Khoja withdrew to a quiet place, where he would be undisturbed, that he might try if he could bite his own ear. Taking the ear in his fingers, he made many efforts to seize it with his teeth, crying, "Can I bite it?"

But in the vehemence of his efforts the Khoja lost his balance and fell backwards, wounding his head.

The following day he took his seat with his head bound up in a linen cloth, and the men coming before him related their dispute as before, and cried, "Now, is it possible, O Cadi?"

"O, you fellows!" said the Khoja, "biting is easy enough, and you can fall and break your own head into the bargain."

Tale 13.—The Khoja's Quilt.

One night after Khoja Nasr-ed-Deen had retired to rest he was disturbed by a man making a great noise before his door in the street outside.

"O wife!" said he, "get up, I pray you, and light a candle, that I may discover what this noise in the street is about."

"Lie still, man," said his wife. "What have we to do with street brawlers? Keep quiet and go to sleep."

But the Khoja would not listen to her advice, and taking the bed-quilt, he threw it round his shoulders, and went out to see what was the matter.

Then the rascal who was making the disturbance, seeing a fine quilt floating from the Khoja's shoulders, came behind him and snatched it away, and ran off with it.

After a while the Khoja felt thoroughly chilled, and he went back to bed.

"Well, Effendi," said his wife: "what have you discovered?"

"We were more concerned in the noise than you thought," said the Khoja.

"What was it about, O Khoja?" asked his wife.

"It must have been about our quilt," he replied; "for when the man got that he went off quietly enough."

Tale 14.—The Khoja and the Beggar.

One day whilst Nasr-ed-Deen Effendi was in his house, a man knocked at the door.

The Khoja looked out from an upper window.

"What dost thou want?" said he. But the man was a beggar by trade, and fearing that the Khoja might refuse to give alms when he was so well beyond reach of the mendicant's importunities, he would not state his business, but continued to cry, "Come down, come down!" as if he had something of importance to relate.

So the Khoja went down, and on his again saying "What dost thou want?" the beggar began to beg, crying, "The Inciter of Compassion move thee to enable me to purchase food for my supper! I am the guest of the Prophet!" with other exclamations of a like nature.

"Come up-stairs," replied the Khoja, turning back into his house.

Well pleased, the beggar followed him, but when they reached the upper room the Khoja turned round and dismissed him, saying, "Heaven supply your necessities. I have nothing for you."

"O Effendi!" said the beggar, "why did you not tell me this whilst I was below?"

"O Beggar!" replied the Khoja, "why did you call me down when I was up-stairs?"

Tale 15.—The Khoja Turned Nightingale.

One day the Khoja went into a garden which did not belong to him, and seeing an apricot-tree laden with delicious fruit,

Juliana Horatia Ewing

he climbed up among the branches and began to help himself.

Whilst he was eating the apricots the owner of the garden came in and discovered him.

"What are you doing up there, Khoja?" said he.

"O my soul!" said the Khoja, "I am not the person you imagine me to be. Do you not see that I am a nightingale? I am singing in the apricot-tree."

"Let me hear you sing," said the gardener.

The Khoja began to trill like a bird; but the noise he made was so uncouth that the man burst out laughing.

"What kind of a song is this?" said he. "I never heard a nightingale's note like that before."

"It is not the voice of a native songster," said the Khoja demurely, "but the foreign nightingale sings so."

Tale 16.—The Khoja's Donkey and The Woollen Pelisse.

One day the Khoja mounted his donkey to ride to the garden, but on the way there he had business which obliged him to dismount and leave the donkey for a short time.

When he got down he took off his woollen pelisse, and throwing it over the saddle, went about his affairs. But he had hardly turned his back when a thief came by who stole the woollen pelisse, and made off with it.

When the Khoja returned and found that the pelisse was gone, he became greatly enraged, and beat the donkey with his stick. Then, dragging the saddle from the poor beast's back, he put it on his own shoulders, crying, "Find my pelisse, you careless rascal, and then you shall have your saddle again!"

Tale 17.—A Ladder To Sell.

There was a certain garden into which the Khoja was desirous to enter, but the gate was fastened, and he could not.

One day, therefore, he took a ladder upon his shoulder, and repaired to the place, where he put the ladder against the garden-wall, and having climbed to the top, drew the ladder over, and by this means descended into the garden.

As he was prying about in came the gardener.

"Who are you?" said he to the Khoja. "And what do you want?"

"I sell ladders," replied the Khoja, running hastily back to the wall, and throwing the ladder once more upon his shoulders.

"Come, come!" said the gardener, "that answer will not do. This is not a place for selling ladders."

"You must be very ignorant," replied the Khoja gravely, "if you do not know that ladders are salable anywhere."

Tale 18.—The Cat and the Khoja's Supper.

The Khoja, like many another man, was fond of something nice for his supper.

But no matter how often he bought a piece of liver to make a tasty dish, his wife always gave it away to a certain friend of hers, and when the Khoja came home in the evening he got nothing to eat but cakes.

"Wife," said he at last, "I bring home some liver every day that we may have a good supper, and you put nothing but pastry before me. What becomes of the meat?"

"The cat steals it, O Khoja!" replied his wife.

On this the Khoja rose from his seat, and taking the axe proceeded to lock it up in a box.

"What are you doing with the axe, Khoja?" said his wife.

"I am hiding it from the cat," replied the Khoja. "The sort of cat who steals two pennyworth of liver is not likely to spare an axe worth forty pence."

Tale 19.—The Cadi's Ferejeh.

One day a certain Cadi of Sur-Hissar, being very drunk, lay down in a garden and fell asleep. The Khoja, having gone out for a walk, passed by the spot and saw the Cadi lying dead drunk and senseless, with his ferejeh—or overcoat—half off his back.

It was a very valuable ferejeh, of rich material, and the Khoja took it and went home remarkably well dressed.

When the Cadi recovered his senses he found that his ferejeh was gone. Thereupon he called his officers and commanded them, saying: "On whomsoever ye shall see my ferejeh, bring the fellow before me."

Meanwhile the Khoja wore it openly, and at last the officers took him and brought him before the Cadi.

"O Khoja!" said the Cadi, "how came you by what belongs to me? Where did you find that ferejeh?"

"Most exemplary Cadi," replied the Khoja, "I went out yesterday for a short time before sunset, and as I walked I perceived a disreputable-looking fellow lying shamefully drunk, and exposed to the derision of passers-by in the public gardens. His ferejeh was half off his back, and I said within myself, 'This valuable ferejeh will certainly be stolen, whilst he to whom it belongs is sleeping the sleep of drunkenness. I will therefore take it and wear it, and when the owner has his senses restored to him, he will be able to see and reclaim it.' So I took the ferejeh, and if it be thine, O Cadi, take it!"

"It cannot be my ferejeh, of course," said the Cadi hastily; "though there is a similarity which at first deceived me."

"Then I will keep it till the man claims it," said the Khoja.

And he did so.

Tale 20.—The Two Pans.

One day the Khoja borrowed a big pan of his next-door neighbour.

When he had done with it he put a smaller pan inside it, and carried it back.

"What is this?" said the neighbour.

"It is a young pan," replied the Khoja. "It is the child of your big pan, and therefore belongs to you."

The neighbour laughed in his sleeve.

"If this Khoja is mad," said he, "a sensible man like myself need not refuse to profit by his whims."

So he replied, "It is well, O Khoja! The pan is a very good pan. May its posterity be increased!"

And he took the Khoja's pan as well as his own, and the Khoja departed.

After a few days the Khoja came again to borrow the big pan, which his neighbour lent him willingly, saying to himself, "Doubtless something else will come back in it." But after he had waited two—three—four—and five days, and the Khoja did not return it, the neighbour betook himself to the Khoja's house and asked for his pan.

The Khoja came to the door with a sad countenance.

"Allah preserve you, neighbour!" said he. "May your health be better than that of our departed friend, who will return to you no more. The big pan is dead."

"Nonsense, Khoja Effendi!" said the neighbour, "You know well enough that a pan cannot die."

"You were quite willing to believe that it had had a child," said the Khoja; "it seems odd you cannot believe that it is dead."

Tale 21.—The Day of the Month.

One day Khoja Effendi walked into the bazaar. As he went about among the buyers and sellers, a man came up to him and said, "Is it the third or fourth day of the month to-day?"

"How should I know?" replied the Khoja. "I don't deal in

the moon."

Tale 22.—The Khoja's Dream.

One night when he was asleep the Khoja dreamed that he found nine pieces of money.

"Bountiful heaven!" said he, "let me have been mistaken. I will count them afresh. Let there be ten!" And when he counted them there were ten. Then he said, "Let there be nineteen!" And vehemently contending for nineteen he awoke. But when he was awake and found that there was nothing in his hands, he shut his eyes again, and stretching his hands out said, "Make it nine pieces, I'll not say another word."

Tale 23.—The Old Moon.

One day some of the neighbours said, "Let us ask this Khoja something that will puzzle him, and see what he will say." So they came to the Khoja and said, "The moon is on the wane, Khoja Effendi, and we shall soon have a new one; what will be done with the old moon?"

"They will break it up and make stars of it," said the Khoja.

Tale 24.—The Short Piece of Muslin.

One day Nasr-ed-Deen Effendi was tying a new piece of muslin for his turban, when to his annoyance he discovered that it was too short. He tried a second time, but still it was not long enough, and he spoiled his turban, and lost his temper. Much vexed with the muslin, the Khoja took it to the bazaar, and gave it in to be sold by auction.

By and by the sale began, and after a time the muslin was put up, and a man came forward and began to bid. Another man bid against him, and the first man continued to raise his price.

The Khoja was standing near, and at last he could bear it no longer. "That rascal of a muslin has cheated me and put me to infinite inconvenience," said he; "it played me false; and am I bound to conceal its deficiencies?"

Then he came softly up to the highest bidder, and whispered, "Take care what you are about, brother, in buying that muslin. It's a short length."

Tale 25.—The Khoja Peeps Into Futurity.

Having need of a stout piece of wood, the Khoja one day decided to cut off a certain branch from a tree that belonged to him, as he perceived that it would serve his purpose.

Taking, therefore, his axe in his hand, and tucking his skirts into his girdle, he climbed the tree, and the branch he desired being firm and convenient, he seated himself upon it, and then began to hack and hew.

As he sat and chopped a man passed by below him, who called out and said, "O stupid man! What are you doing? When the branch is cut through you will certainly fall to the ground."

"Are the decrees of the future less veiled from this man than from me, who am a Khoja?" said Nasr-ed-Deen Effendi to himself, and he made the man no reply, but chopped on.

In a few moments the branch gave way, and the Khoja fell to the ground.

When he recovered himself he jumped up, and ran after the man who had warned him.

"O you fellow!" cried he. "It has happened to me even as you foretold. At the moment when the branch was cut through I fell to the ground. Now, therefore, since the future is open to thee, I beseech thee to tell me the day of my death."

"This madness is greater than the other," replied the man. "The day of death is among the hidden counsels of the Most High."

But the Khoja held him by the gown and continued to urge him, saying, "You told me when I should fall from the tree, and it came to pass to the moment. Tell me now how long I have to live." And as he would not release him, but kept crying, "How much time have I left?" the man lost patience, and said, "O fool! there is no more time left to thee. The days of the years of thy life are numbered."

"Then I am dead, lo I am dead!" said the Khoja, and he lay down, and stiffened himself, and did not move.

By and by his neighbours came and stood at his head, and having observed him, they brought a bier and laid him on it, saying, "Let us take him to his own house."

Now in the way thither there was in the road a boggy place, which it was difficult to pass, and the bearers of the bier stood still and consulted, saying, "Which way shall we go?"

And they hesitated so long that the Khoja, becoming impatient, raised his head from the bier, and said, "*That's* the way I used to go myself, when I was alive."

Tale 26.—The Two Moons.

On a certain day when the Khoja went to Sur-Hissar he saw a group of persons looking at the new moon.

"What extraordinary people the men of this place must be!" said he, "In our country the moon may be seen as large as a plate, and no one troubles his head about it, and here people stare at it when it is only a quarter the size."

Tale 27.—The Khoja Preaching.

One of the Khoja's duties—as a religious teacher—was to preach to the people. But once upon a time he became very lazy about this, and was always seeking an excuse to shorten or omit his sermons.

On a certain day about this time he mounted into the pulpit, and looking down on the congregation assembled to listen to him, he stretched forth his hands and cried, "Ah, Believers! what shall I say to you?"

And the men beat upon their breasts, and replied with one voice, "We do not know, most holy Khoja! we do not know."

"Oh, if you don't know—" said the Khoja indignantly, and gathering his robe about him, he quitted the pulpit without another word.

The men looked at each other in dismay, for the Khoja was a very popular preacher.

"We have done wrong," said they, "though we know not how; without doubt our ignorance is an offence to his learning. Wherefore, if he comes again, whatever he says to us we will seem as if we knew all about it."

The following week the Khoja got again into the pulpit, from which he could see a larger assembly than before.

"O ye Muslims!" he began, "what am I to say—"

But before the words were fairly out of his mouth the congregation cried out with one voice, "*We* know, good Khoja! We know!"

"Oh, if you *know*—" said the Khoja sarcastically, and shrugging his shoulders, and lifting his eyebrows, he left the place as one who feels that he can be of no further use.

"This is worse than before," said the Muslims in despair. But after a while they took counsel, and said, "Let him come once more, and we will not lose our sermon this time. If he asks the same question we will reply that some of us know, but that some of us do not know."

So when the Khoja next appeared before the congregation, and after he had cried as before, "O Brethren! do ye know what I am about to say?" they answered, "Some of us know, but some of us do not know."

"How nice!" said the Khoja, smiling benevolently upon the crowd beneath him, as he prepared to take his departure. "Then those of you who know can explain it all to those who do not know."

Tale 28.—The Khoja and the Horsemen.

One day when Khoja Effendi was crossing a certain desert plain a troop of horsemen suddenly appeared riding towards him.

"No doubt these are Bedawee robbers," thought the Khoja, "who will kill me without remorse for the sake of the Cadi's ferejeh which I wear." And in much alarm he hastened towards a cemetery which he had perceived to be near. Here he quickly stripped off his clothes, and, having hidden them, crept naked into an empty tomb and lay down.

But the horsemen pursued after him, and by and by they came into the cemetery, and one of them peeped into the tomb and saw the Khoja.

"Here is the man we saw!" cried the horseman; and he said to the Khoja, "What are you lying there for, and where are your clothes?"

"The dead have no possessions, O Bedawee!" replied the Khoja. "I am buried here. If you saw me on the plain as I used to appear in life, without doubt you are one of those who can see ghosts and apparitions."

Tale 29.—The Ox Trespassing.

One day Khoja Effendi, repairing to a piece of ground which belonged to him, found that a strange ox had got into the enclosure. The Khoja took a thick stick to beat it with, but the beast, seeing him coming, ran away and escaped.

Next week the Khoja met a Turk driving the ox, which was harnessed to a waggon.

Thereupon the Khoja took a stick in his hand, and, running after the ox, belaboured it soundly. "O man!" cried the Turk, "what are you beating my beast for?"

"Hold your tongue, you fool," said the Khoja, "and don't meddle with what doesn't concern you. *The ox knows well enough.*"

Tale 30.—The Khoja's Camel.

The next time Khoja Effendi was obliged to take a journey he resolved to accompany a caravan for protection.

Now the Khoja had lately become possessed of a valuable camel, and he said to himself, "I will ride my camel instead of going on foot; the journey will then be a pleasure, and I shall not be fatigued." So he mounted the camel and set forth.

But as he was riding with the caravan the camel stumbled, and the Khoja was thrown off and severely hurt. The people of the caravan coming to his assistance found that he was stunned, but after a while they succeeded in restoring him.

When the Khoja came to his senses he tore his clothes, and cried in great rage and indignation, "O Muslims! you do not know what care I have taken of this camel, and this is how I am rewarded! Will no one kill it for me? It has done its best to kill me."

But his friends said, "Be appeased, most worthy Effendi, we could not kill your valuable camel."

"O benefactors!" replied the Khoja, "since you desire the brute's life it must be spared. But it shall have no home with me. I am about to drive it into the desert, where it may stumble to its heart's content."

So the Khoja drove the camel away; but before he did so he tore the furniture and trappings furiously from its back, crying, "I won't leave you a rag, you ungrateful beast!"

And he pursued his journey on foot, carrying the camel's furniture as best as he might.

Juliana Horatia Ewing

Tale 31.—An Open Question.

The Khoja wanted vegetables for cooking, so he took a sack and slipped into a neighbouring garden, which was abundantly supplied. He picked some herbs, and pulled up some turnips, and got a little of everything he could find to fill his bag. Both hands were full, when the gardener suddenly appeared and seized him.

"What are you doing here?" said the gardener.

The Khoja was confounded, and not being able to find a good excuse, he said, "A very strong wind blew during the night. Having driven me a long way, it blew me here."

"Oh," said the gardener; "but who plucked these herbs which I see in your hands?"

"The wind was so very strong," answered the Khoja, "that when it blew me into this place I clutched with both hands at the first things I could lay hold of, lest it should drive me further. And so they remain in my grasp."

"Oh," said the gardener; "but who put these into the sack, I wonder?"

"That is just what puzzles me," the Khoja replied; "I was thinking about it when you came in."

Tale 32.—The Spurting Fountain.

One summer's day the Khoja had come a long way, and was very hot and thirsty. By and by he perceived a fountain, of which the pipe was stopped up with a piece of wood.

"Now I shall quench my thirst," said the Khoja, and he

pulled out the stopper, on which the water rushed out with vehement force over the Khoja's head, and drenched him in a moment.

"Ah!" cried the Khoja angrily, "it's because of your running so madly that they have stuck that stick into you, I suppose."

Tale 33.—Well-meant Soup.

One day as the Khoja was returning home he met a party of students walking together.

"Good-evening, Effendis!" said he. "Pray come home with me, and we will have some soup."

The students did not think twice about accepting the invitation, and they followed the Khoja home to his house.

"Pray be seated," said the Khoja, and when they had seated themselves he went to the upper room. "Wife," said he, "I have brought home some guests. Let us give them a good bowl of soup."

"O Effendi!" cried the wife, "is there any butter in the house? Is there any rice? Have you brought anything home for me to make it of, that you ask for soup?"

"Give me the soup-bowl," said the Khoja. Then taking the empty bowl in his hand he returned to the students.

"O Effendis!" said he, "be good enough, I beseech you, to take the will for the deed. You are indeed most welcome, and if there had been butter or rice, or anything else in our house, you would have had excellent soup out of this very bowl."

Tale 34.—The Khoja and the Ten Blind Men.

Once upon a time Khoja Nasr-ed-Deen, wandering by the banks of a river, came to a certain ford near which he seated himself to rest.

By and by came ten blind men, who were desirous of crossing the river, and they agreed with the Khoja that he should help them across for the payment of one penny each.

The Khoja accordingly exerted himself to the utmost of his power, and he got nine of the blind men safely across; but as he was helping the tenth, the man lost his footing, and in spite of the Khoja's efforts the river overpowered him, and bore him away.

Thereupon the nine blind men on the opposite shore set up a lamentable wail, crying, "What has happened, O Khoja?"

"One penny less to pay than you expected," said the Khoja.

Tale 35.—The End of the World.

Now Khoja Nasr-ed-Deen Effendi had a lamb which he brought up and fattened with much care.

Some of his friends were very desirous to get hold of this lamb and make a feast of it. So they came to the Khoja and begged him earnestly to give up the lamb for a feast, but the Khoja would not consent.

At last one day came one of them and said, "O Khoja! to-morrow is the end of the world. What will you do with this lamb on the last day? We may as well eat it this evening."

"If it be so, let us do as you say," replied the Khoja, for he thought that the man was in earnest. So they lighted the fire and roasted the lamb, and had an excellent feast. But the

Khoja perceived that they had played a trick upon him.

By and by his friends went to some little distance to play games together, but the Khoja would not accompany them, so they left their upper garments in his charge and departed to their amusements.

When they were gone the Khoja took the clothes and put them on to the fire where the lamb had been roasted, and burnt them all.

After a while the friends returned and found their robes burnt to ashes.

"O Khoja!" they cried, "who has burnt our clothes? Alas, alas! what shall we do?"

"Never mind," said the Khoja, "to-morrow the world comes to an end, you know. You would not have wanted them for long."

Tale 36.—The Dog on the Tomb.

One day the Khoja was wandering among the tombs. As he strolled along he perceived a dog lying upon a grave-stone.

Indignant at this profanation of a tomb, the Khoja took a stout stick and made up his mind to chastise the intruder. But the dog, who saw what was coming, got up and prepared to fly at him.

The Khoja never ran any unnecessary risk. When he perceived that the dog was about to attack him, and that he would have the worst of it, he lowered his stick.

"Pray don't disturb yourself," said he; "I give in."

Tale 37.—The Khoja and the Mullas.

Once upon a time the Khoja, riding on his donkey, was proceeding to a certain place to give public instruction, when he was followed by several law-students, who walked behind him.

Perceiving this, the Khoja dismounted, and got up again with his face to the donkey's tail.

"O Khoja!" cried the Mullas, "why do you ride backwards?"

"It is the only way in which we can show each other proper civility," replied the Khoja; "for when I ride in the usual fashion, if you walk behind me I turn my back on you, and if you walk before me you turn your backs on me."

Tale 38.—The Students and the Khoja's Wife.

Khoja Nasr-ed-Deen Effendi met a party of students who were walking together.

"Allow me to join you, worthy Effendis," said he, "and if it is agreeable to you we will proceed to my house."

"With the greatest possible pleasure," replied all the students, and the Khoja, beguiling the way with smart sayings and agreeable compliments, led them to the door of his dwelling.

"Be good enough to wait an instant," said the Khoja, and the students waited whilst the Khoja entered his house, where—being in a mischievous mood—he said to his wife, "O wife, go down and send those men away who are hanging about the door. If they want me, say that I have not come home."

So the woman went down and said, "The Khoja has not

come home, gentlemen."

"What are you talking about?" cried the students; "he came home with us."

"He's not at home, I tell you," said the Khoja's wife.

"We know that he is," said the students.

"He's not," repeated the woman.

"He is," reiterated the students.

And so they contradicted each other and bandied words, till the Khoja, who was listening from above, put his head out of the window and cried, "Neither you nor my wife have any sense in your heads. Don't you see there are two doors to the place? If he did come in by one he may have gone out again through the other."

Tale 39.—The Khoja and His Guest.

One day a man came to the Khoja and became his guest for the night.

When they had had supper they lay down to sleep.

After a while the light went out; but the Khoja was lazy, and pretended not to observe it, for he did not want to get up.

"Khoja! Khoja!" cried the guest.

"What's the matter?" said the Khoja.

"Don't you see that the light's gone out?" said the guest.

"I see nothing," said the Khoja.

"It's pitch dark," complained the guest: "do get up and see if you have a candle in the house."

"You must be mad," replied the Khoja; "am I a cat? If it is really as dark as you say how can I possibly see whether I have got any or not?"

Tale 40.—The Wise Donkey.

Once upon a time the Khoja was smoking in his garden, when a certain man came to borrow his donkey.

Now this man was cruel to animals, therefore the Khoja did not like to lend him his beast; but as he was also a man of some consideration, the Khoja hesitated to refuse point blank.

"O Effendi!" said he, "I will gladly lend you my donkey, but he is a very wise animal, and knows what is about to befall him. If he foresees good luck for this journey all will be well, and you could not have a better beast. But if he foresees evil he will be of no use, and I should be ashamed to offer him to you."

"Be good enough to inquire of him," said the borrower.

Thereupon the Khoja departed on pretence of taking counsel with his donkey. But he only smoked another pipe in his garden, and then returned to the man, who was anxiously awaiting him, and whom he saluted with all possible politeness, saying—

"May it be far from you, most worthy Effendi, ever to experience such misfortune as my wise donkey foresees on this occasion!"

"What does he foresee?" inquired the borrower.

"Broken knees, sore ribs, aching bones, long marches, and short meals," said the Khoja.

Then the man looked foolish, and sneaked away without reply.

But the Khoja went back to his pipe.

Tale 41.—The Khoja's Horse.

Once upon a time the Khoja was travelling in company with a caravan, when they halted for the night at a certain place, and all the horses were tied up together.

Next morning the Khoja could not for the life of him remember which was his own horse, and he was much afraid of being cheated if he confessed this to the rest.

So, as they were all coming out, he seized his bow and arrow, and aimed among the horses at random.

"Don't shoot!" cried the men; "what is the matter?"

"I am desperate," replied the Khoja; "I am determined to kill somebody's horse, so let every one look to his own."

Laughing at the Khoja's folly, each man untied his own horse as quickly as possible, and took it away.

Then the Khoja knew that the one left was his own.

He at once proceeded to mount, but putting his right foot into the stirrup, he came round with his face to the tail.

"What makes you get up backwards, Khoja?" said his friends.

"It is not I who am in the wrong," said the Khoja, "but the horse that is left-handed."

Tale 42.—The Khoja on the Bey's Horse.

On a certain occasion Khoja Nasr-ed-Deen went to see the Bey, and the Bey invited him to go out hunting.

The Khoja agreed, but when they were about to start he found that he had been mounted on a horse which would not move out of a snail's pace. He said nothing, however, for it is not well to be too quick in seeing affronts.

By and by it began to rain heavily. The Bey and the rest of the party galloped off with all speed towards shelter, and the Khoja was left in the lurch.

When they were all out of sight the Khoja got down and took off all his clothes and folded them neatly together, and put them on the saddle. Then he got up again and sat on his clothes, to keep them dry.

By and by the rain ceased, and the Khoja dressed himself and went leisurely home. When he reached the Bey's palace all the guests were assembled, and presently the Bey perceived him and cried out, "Why, here is the worthy Khoja! And—how extraordinary!—his clothes are not as wet as ours."

"Why do you not praise the horse on which you mounted me?" answered the Khoja; "it carried me through the storm without a single thread of my clothes being wet."

"They must have made a mistake about the horses," thought the Bey to himself, and he invited the Khoja to go hunting on the following day.

The Khoja accepted, and when the time came he was mounted on the horse which the Bey had ridden the day before, and the Bey seated himself on that which had carried the Khoja with dry clothes through the shower.

By and by it began to rain; every one rode off as usual, and this time the Khoja among them.

The Bey, however, could not induce his horse to stir out of a foot's pace, and when he arrived at his palace he was drenched to the skin.

"Wretched man!" he cried to the Khoja, "is it not through you that I was induced to ride this useless horse?"

"Most eminent Bey," replied the Khoja, "the beast has treated you no worse than he served me. But perhaps your Eminence did not think of taking off your clothes and sitting on them?"

Tale 43.—The Khoja's Donkey brays to Good Purpose.

One day the Khoja dismounted at the door of a shop, and threw his woollen pelisse on the donkey's back till he should return. He then went in to buy sweetmeats.

In a few minutes there passed a man, who snatched the woollen pelisse from the donkey's back, and went off with it. At this moment the donkey began to bray.

"O bawl away!" cried the Khoja, who had come out just in time to see his pelisse disappear; "much good that will do."

But as it happened, when the man heard the noise he was afraid of being caught, and, throwing the pelisse back on to the donkey, he ran away as hard as he could.

Tale 44.—The Khoja's Left Leg.

During one very hot season there was a scarcity of water in the city.

One day, the Khoja was performing his religious ablutions: he washed himself all over with the exception of his left leg, but before that could be washed the water was all used up.

When the Khoja began to recite the customary prayers he stood on one leg like a goose.

"O Khoja Effendi!" cried the people, "why do you pray standing on your right leg?"

"I could not pray on my left leg," said the Khoja; "it has not performed the appointed ablutions."

Tale 45.—"Figs Would Be More Acceptable."

Nasr-ed-Deen Effendi had some plums, of which he resolved to make a present to the Bey. He therefore took three of them, and putting them on a fine tray, he carried them into the royal presence, and duly offered them for the Bey's acceptance.

Being in a good humour, the Bey took the present in good part, and gave the Khoja several pence in return.

After some days the Khoja thought he would take something else to the Bey, and having some fine large beetroots, he set off as before.

On his way to the palace he met a man, who saluted him.

"What are you doing with all those beetroots?" said he.

"I am about to present them to the Bey," replied the Khoja.

"Figs would be more acceptable, I should think," said the man.

The Khoja pursued his journey, but as he went the man's words troubled him—"Figs would be more acceptable."

At last he perceived a fig-tree by the roadside, so, throwing away all the beetroots, he put two or three figs in their place, and having arrived at the palace, he presented them to the Bey.

But this time the Bey was not in a good humour.

"What madman is this," he cried, "who mocks me by the gift of a few worthless figs? Throw them at his head and drive him away!"

So they pelted the Khoja with his figs, and drove him out. But as he ran, instead of cursing his ill luck, the Khoja gave thanks for his good fortune.

"This is indeed madness," cried the servants of the Bey; "for what, O Khoja, do you return thanks, after this ignominious treatment?"

"O ignorant time-servers," replied the Khoja, "I have good

reason to give thanks. For I was bringing beetroots to the Bey—large beetroots, and many of them—and I met a man who persuaded me, saying, "Figs would be more acceptable," so I brought figs; and you have cast them at my head. But there were few of them, and they are soft, and I am none the worse. If, however, I had not by good luck thrown away the beetroots, which are hard, my skull would certainly have been cracked."

Tale 46.—Timur and the One-legged Geese.

One day the Khoja caused a goose to be cooked. He was about to present it to the King.

When it was nicely done he set off with it, but on the road he became very hungry. If the smell of it were to be trusted it was a most delicious bird! At last the Khoja could resist no longer, and he tore off a leg and ate it with much relish.

On arriving in the royal presence he placed the goose before Timur the King, who, when he had examined the Khoja's gift, was exceedingly annoyed.

"This Khoja is deriding me!" said he. And then in a voice of thunder he demanded, "*Where is the other leg?*"

"The geese of our country are one-legged," replied Nasr-ed-Deen, with much gravity. "If your Majesty does not believe me, be good enough to let your eyes be informed of the truth of what I say by looking at the geese at yonder spring."

As it happened there were a number of geese at the fountain, and they were all standing on one leg.

The King could not help laughing, but he called to his drummers and said, "March towards yonder fountain, and lay your drumsticks well about your drums."

The drummers forthwith began to drum, and they rattled away so heartily that all the geese put down their legs and ran off in alarm.

"O Khoja!" cried Timur, "how is this? All your geese have become two-legged!"

"It is the effect of your Majesty's wonderful drumsticks," replied the Khoja. "If you were to eat one of them, you yourself would undoubtedly become four-legged."

Tale 47.—The Khoja Rewards the Frogs.

Khoja Nasr-ed-Deen Effendi had been riding his donkey for some miles. It was very hot, and the Khoja dismounted to ease his beast. At this moment they came within sight of a pond, and the donkey smelling the water set off towards it as hard as he could canter.

The side of the pond was very steep, and in its haste the donkey would probably have fallen in, but that the frogs set up such a terrific croaking at its approach that the beast, in alarm, turned sharply round, and was caught by its master.

The Khoja was not wanting in grateful and liberal feelings.

"Well done, my little pond-birds!" said he, throwing a handful of coins into the water. "Divide that among you to buy sweetmeats with."

Tale 48.—The Khoja reproaches his Cock.

Once upon a time the Khoja was carrying his fowls in a cage to the city for sale.

Juliana Horatia Ewing

As he went along he began to feel sorry for them.

"O my soul!" said he, "these poor fowls are sadly imprisoned. I will let them go a little." So he opened the cage, and the birds scrambled out. One ran one way, and another another; but the Khoja contrived to keep up with the cock, which he drove before him with his stick, the poor bird waddling hither and thither, and fluttering from side to side with distress and indecision pitiable to behold.

On seeing this the Khoja began to reproach him. "You never thought it would come to this, my fine bird, did you?" said he. "And yet what a wiseacre you are! You know when it's day better than the sun himself, and can crow loud enough for all the world to hear your wisdom."

The poor cock made no reply, but waddled on with hoarse cries and flapping wings.

"You're a poor prophet!" said the Khoja. "You know that it is morning in the middle of the night: how is it you could not foresee that you were to be driven to market? Thus—and thus!" And turning him at every corner by which he would escape, the Khoja drove the distracted cock into the city.

Tale 49.—Hare-soup.

One day there came a man from the village who made the Khoja a present of a hare.

The Khoja brought him in, treating him with all honour and hospitality, and gave him some rich and excellent soup.

In a week's time the man called again; but the Khoja had forgotten him, and said, "Who are you?"

"I am the man who brought the hare," he replied. The Khoja entertained him as before, though the soup was not quite so rich.

After a few days came some men who desired to be guests to the Khoja.

"Who are you?" said he.

"We are neighbours of the man who brought the hare," said they.

This time the soup was certainly thin, but that did not hinder the arrival of some fresh guests in a very few days.

"Who are you?" said the Khoja.

"We are neighbours of the neighbours of the man who brought the hare," was the reply.

"You are welcome," said their host; and he set a bowl of clear water before them.

"What is this, O Khoja?" cried the men.

"It is soup of soup of soup of the hare-soup," answered the Khoja.

Tale 50.—The Khoja out Fishing.

One day the Khoja accompanied some men who were going a-fishing, and he became much excited in watching the sport.

Suddenly, as they cast the net into the sea, the Khoja threw himself into it.

"What can you be thinking of, Effendi?" cried the fishermen.

"I forgot," said the Khoja; "I was thinking I was a fish."

Tale 51.—A Desire Satisfied.

Nasr-ed-Deen Effendi had an old cow with horns so exceedingly broad that one could certainly sit between them if he had a mind to do so.

"I should very much like to try," the Khoja kept thinking; "I should exceedingly like to sit for once between those horns."

The notion haunted him, and he kept saying to himself, "I certainly should like it, just for once."

One day the cow came before the house, and after a while lay down.

"The opportunity has arrived," cried the Khoja, and running out, he seated himself between the cow's horns. "It is just as I thought," said he; but as he spoke the cow got up, and tossed the Khoja violently to the ground.

The Khoja was stunned, and when his wife hastened to the spot she found him lying senseless. After some time he opened his eyes, and perceived his wife weeping near him.

"O wife!" said the Khoja, "weep not; I am not less fortunate than other men. I have suffered for it, but I have had my desire."

Tale 52.—The Khoja and the Incompetent Barber.

On one occasion the Khoja was shaved by a most incompetent barber. At every stroke the man cut his head with the razor, and kept sticking on bits of cotton to stop the bleeding.

At last the Khoja lost patience.

"That will do," said he, jumping up: "you've sown cotton on half my head, I'll keep the other half for flax;" and he ran out of the shop with his head half shaved.

FOOTNOTES:

[Footnote 3: A *Khoja* is a religious teacher, and sometimes a school-master also.]

THE SNARLING PRINCESS

(Freely adapted from the German.)

Ever so long ago there lived a certain king, at whose court great rejoicings were held for the birth of a child. But this joy was soon turned to sorrow, when the young queen died, and left her infant daughter motherless. As the body of the young queen lay in state, wrapped in a shroud of gold all embroidered with flowers, and with so sweet a smile upon her face that she looked like one who dreams happy dreams in sleep, the sorrowing king took the child in his arms, and kneeling by the bier vowed never to marry again, but to make his wife's only child the heir of his crown and kingdom. This promise he faithfully fulfilled, and remaining a widower, he devoted his life to the upbringing of his daughter.

It is true that the young princess had a fairy godmother—a distant cousin of the deceased queen—but the king could not endure that any one but himself should have a voice in the management of his child, and the fairy godmother, who was accustomed to the utmost deference to her opinions, very soon quitted the court in a huff, and left the king as supreme in the nursery as he was in the council-chamber.

When the precious baby was washed, this was done with no

common care. The bath itself was made of gold, and the two chief physicians of the kingdom assisted the king by their counsels. When hot water of crystal clearness had been poured into the bath, the more celebrated of the two physicians dipped the tip of his little finger in, and looking inquiringly at his colleague, said "*Hum*." On which the physician of lesser degree dipped in his little finger and said "*Hem*." And after this the water always proved to be of the right temperature, and did the young princess no harm whatever. The king himself on these occasions always dropped—with much state—a few drops of exquisite scent into the bath, from a golden flask studded with diamonds. The chief lady-in-waiting brought the baby, wrapped in gorgeous robes, and put it into the bath. The court doctors laid their fingers on their noses, and looked very important, whilst the king—who was short-sighted—put on his spectacles to enjoy the sight of the little princess, who gambolled in the water like a fish. The rest of her toilette was carried out with no less formality, and as the same scrupulous care watched over every incident of her daily life, the child grew every day more healthy and beautiful.

Time passed on without lessening the king's devotion to his daughter. Her beauty was the standing theme of conversation in every corner of the palace where the king was likely to overhear it, and the courtiers rivalled each other in trying to read the wishes of the little princess in her blue eyes, and in endeavouring to forestall them.

No wonder the little lady grew up exceedingly self-willed, and with no thought of any one's pleasure but her own.

The king hired governesses, it is true, but he strictly forbade them ever to say a harsh word to his darling; and one who had so far transgressed this order as to reprove the princess for some fault, was dismissed in disgrace. Thus it came about that the child grew daily more and more wilful and capricious. Do what every one would, it was impossible to please her, and as she was allowed to fly into a rage about the most trifling matters, and as she sulked and scolded, and growled and grumbled for the smallest annoyances, her voice gradually acquired a peculiar snarling tone, which was as painful to listen to as it was unbecoming in a young and pretty princess.

The whole court suffered from the depressing effects of the young lady's ill-temper. Behind the king's back, the courtiers complained pretty freely, but before his face no one dared show his annoyance, and two old court ladies, whose nerves were not so strong as they had been, and who feared to betray themselves, were obliged to employ a celebrated professor of cosmetics to paint smiles on their faces that could not be disturbed by the snarling and grumbling of the princess; but the Lord Chamberlain concealed his feelings by a free use of his gold snuff-box, and snuffed away his annoyance pretty successfully.

As his daughter grew up, the king was not without his share of suffering from her ill-temper. But he bore it all very patiently,—"She will be a queen," said he to himself, "and it is fit that she should have a will of her own." The king himself was of an imperious temper, but such was his love for his only child, that he bent it completely to her caprices.

In private, the courtiers were by no means so indulgent in their views, and the future queen was known amongst them, behind her back, as the Snarling Princess.

In spite of her ill-temper and unpleasing voice, however, she was so beautiful, that—being also heir to the throne of a large kingdom—many princes sought her hand in marriage. But the Snarling Princess was resolved to reign alone, and she refused every suitor who appeared.

The princess's rooms were, of course, the most beautiful in the palace. One of these, which looked out on to the forest, was her favourite chamber, but it was also the source of her greatest vexation.

Never did she look out of the window towards the wood without snarling in her harshest tone, "Hateful! Intolerable!"

The source of her annoyance was this:

On the edge of the forest, clearly to be seen from her window, there stood a tiny cottage, in which lived an aged woman who was known amongst the poor folks of the neighbourhood as the "Three-legged Wood-wife." This was because of a wooden staff on which she leaned to eke out the failing strength of her own limbs. The wood-wife was both feared and hated by the people, amongst whom she bore the character of a very malicious witch. The king's daughter hated not only her, but her tumble-down house, and had sent again and again, with large offers of gold, to try and purchase the cottage. But the wood-wife laughed spitefully at the messengers, and only replied that the cottage suited her, and that for no money would she quit it whilst she lived.

The poor have their rights, however, as well as the rich, and even the Snarling Princess was obliged to submit to the disappointment at which she could only grumble.

At one time she resolved never to go into her favourite room again. But she could not keep her resolution. Back she went, and some irresistible power always seemed to draw her to the window to irritate herself by the sight of the wretched hovel which belonged to the Three-legged Witch.

At last, however, by constantly snarling and complaining to the king, she induced him to turn the old woman by force out of her cottage. The king, who was just and upright, did so very unwillingly, and he built her a new and much better cottage elsewhere.

The wood-wife could not resist, but she never put her foot across the threshold of the new house. Meanwhile the old hovel was swept away as fast as possible, and by the princess's wish a pretty summer-house was built on the spot where it had stood, and there she and her court ladies were wont to amuse themselves on warm summer evenings to their hearts' content.

One evening the princess strolled out by herself into the forest. She had been in several distinct rages; first with her court ladies, secondly with her dressmaker, thirdly with the sky, which, in spite of her wishes for fine weather, had become overcast with clouds.

In this ill-humour nothing in all the beautiful green forest gave her any satisfaction. She snarled at the birds because they sang so merrily. The rustling of the green fir-tops in the evening breeze annoyed her: "Why should pine-trees have needles instead of leaves?" she asked angrily; and then she grumbled because there were no roses on the juniper bushes. Still snarling, she wandered on, till she came to a spot where she stood still and silent in sheer amazement.

In an open space there was a circle of grotesque-looking stones, strangely linked together by creeping plants and ferns of curious growth. And as the Snarling Princess looked at them, it seemed to her that the stones took dwarf-like shapes, and glared about them with weird elfin faces. The princess seemed rooted to the spot. An invisible power appeared to draw her towards the group, and to attract her by a beautiful flower, whose calyx opened at her approach. Unable to resist the impulse, she stepped into the circle and plucked the flower.

No sooner had she done so than her feet took deep root in the earth, her hair stiffened into fir-needles, and her arms became branches. She was now firmly fixed in the centre of the group of stones, a slender, swaying pine-tree, which creaked and croaked, and snapped and snarled with every gust of wind, as the princess had hardly ever done in her most ill-tempered moments. And as her limbs stiffened under their magical transformation, the hideous figure of the wood-wife might have been seen hovering round the charmed circle, her arms half changed into bird's wings, and her hands into claws. And as the king's daughter fairly turned into a pine-tree, the wood-wife took the form of an owl, and for a moment rested triumphantly on her branches. Then with a shrill "Tu-whit! tu-whoo!" it vanished into the forest.

When the princess did not return to the palace, and all search after her proved utterly vain, the poor old king fell into a state of the deepest melancholy, and spent most of his time in the summer-house, bewailing the mysterious loss of his only child.

One day, many months afterwards, he wandered into the forest. A storm was raging, of which he took no heed. But suddenly he stopped beneath a pine-tree, and looked up—"How like my poor dear daughter's voice!" said he; "especially when she was the least bit in the world—" He did not like to finish the sentence, but sat down under the tree and wept bitterly. And for every tear he shed, the pine-tree dropped a shower of needles. For the Snarling Princess recognized her father, and heartily lamented the pain he suffered now, and had so often suffered before on her account.

"Tu-whit! tu-whoo!" said a voice, from a hole beneath the pine-tree.

"Who speaks?" said the king.

"It is I, cousin," said the owl, hopping into the daylight, and gradually assuming the form and features of the fairy godmother. "You did not know me as the Three-legged Wood-wife, whom you so unjustly sacrificed to your daughter's caprices. But I have had a hand in her education after all! For twelve months has she croaked and creaked, snapped and snarled, beneath the summer heat, the winter snow, and the storms of spring and autumn. Her punishment—and yours—is over."

As the fairy godmother spoke, the pine-tree became a princess once more, and fell into her father's arms.

But the wood-wife took again the shape of an owl, and the enchanted stones became bats, and they all disappeared into the shadows of the forest.

And as the princess shortly afterwards married a very charming prince, she no doubt changed her name.

Certainly she was never more known as the Snarling Princess.

THE LITTLE PARSNIP-MAN

(Freely adapted from the German.)

WHAT PETER FOUND IN THE PAN—AN UGLY SMILE—THE WIDOW'S RECKONINGS—REST BY RUSHLIGHT.

On a cold winter's evening it is very cosy to sit by a warm hearth, where the fire crackles pleasantly, and the old saucepan, which Mother has set on the fire, sings monotonously to itself between-whiles.

On such a night the wind howled in the street without, beat upon the window-panes, and rustled through the trees, which stood, tall and leafless, in the big garden over the way.

Little Peter did not trouble his head on the subject. He sat indoors on a little footstool, near the fire, and close also to his mother, who was busy cutting up parsnips for next day's dinner.

Peter paid great attention as his mother took a well-boiled parsnip out of the saucepan, scraped it, cut it, and laid the pieces on a clean white dish.

Juliana Horatia Ewing

His mother's thoughts were elsewhere. She looked sad and pensive. Only from time to time she nodded across the dish towards her little Peter, and when he got up and came and laid his head in her lap, she gently smoothed his fair hair from his brow, and then she smiled too.

Peter had no idea that his mother was sad. He had got another parsnip out of the pan, and wanted to scrape it all by himself; but he was not very skilful, and he worked so slowly that in the end his mother had to finish it for him.

The next thing he did was to upset the saucepan; the parsnips fell out, and Peter began to count them.

All at once he gave a cry that made his mother jump. He had found a parsnip-root that looked exactly like a little man. It had a regular head of its own, with a long nose, its body was short, and it had two shrivelled stringy little legs; arms it had none.

"That's a little Parsnip-man," said his mother, when Peter showed it to her.

"A Parsnip-man?" muttered Peter below his breath, and he gazed doubtfully at the odd-looking root in his hand.

It seemed to him that the little man was smiling at him; but with a very ugly kind of smile.

Suddenly the stove gave such a loud crack, that Peter let the parsnip fall out of his hands with a start.

"What's the matter?" asked his mother, as Peter buried his face in her arms; for he began to feel frightened.

"The little Parsnip-man grinned so nastily at me, and such a loud noise came out of the stove—and I let him fall!" His mother laughed at him.

"You've been dreaming," said she. "The little man could not smile if he tried. The Parsnip-mannikins are only roots in the day-time, you know. It is at midnight, when you have long, long been asleep, and the church clock strikes twelve, that they come to life. Then away they all go to the great cave where the queen dwells in state, and here they hold high festival. There they dance, sing, play, and eat out of golden dishes. But as soon as the clock strikes one, all is over, and the Parsnip-men are only roots once more.

"But you've fallen asleep," she added. "Come, my child, and I'll put you to bed. You are tired, are you not?"

"Yes, I'll go to bed," said little Peter, rubbing his drowsy eyes. So his mother took him into the bedroom and lighted the rushlight. Then she undressed him and put him to bed. And Peter had hardly touched the pillow before he was fast asleep.

But the mother went back to the kitchen-table, and seated herself once more by the light of the dimly-burning lamp. The parsnips were all cut up long ago. She put the dish aside and began to sew. Now and then she paused in her work to lean back in her chair, and tears welled up in her eyes. Perhaps she remembered that the rent was due, or she may have been reflecting that Peter's jacket was past further patching. In either case she began to count over in her mind a certain small stock of savings which she had laid by in a money-box, and to puzzle her poor head what she should turn her hand to next to earn the wherewithal to buy the boy some decent clothes. Nothing likely suggested itself, however, and with a heavy sigh she bent once more over her work and stitched away faster than ever. For the work she was doing had to be taken home next morning; and there was a great deal yet to do if she hoped to get it finished in time, and to pay her rent with the price of it.

After sitting like this for a while, she got up. Her eyes ached, and it was getting late. The big kitchen clock was on the stroke of twelve. She put her sewing away in her work-basket, and carried the saucepan and the dish of parsnips into the scullery. Then she swept up the spare roots into a corner of the hearth, and put the little stool tidily away under the table.

But she could not see anything of the parsnip which Peter had let fall. Possibly it had rolled behind the stove.

"I shall be sure to find it in the morning, when I light the fire," she thought.

She put out the lamp, and stepped softly into the chamber where the rushlight burned dimly. Then with one passing glance at the sleeping boy, she undressed herself and prepared for bed.

In a few moments more all her cares and troubles had vanished in slumber.

THE LITTLE MAN IN THE YELLOW COAT—A MOUSE-RIDE AT MIDNIGHT—THE HOLE IN THE WALL—AMONG THE PARSNIP-MEN—QUEEN MARY—THE BLUE DRESS—A CAKE-FEAST—ONE!

Little Peter had been asleep for a long time, when all at once he found himself suddenly twitched by the arm. He rolled over, rubbed his eyes, and then, to his amazement, saw the little Parsnip-man sitting by him on the quilt.

He did not look a bit like a parsnip now. He had on a long yellow coat, and a little green hat on his head; and he nodded in quite a friendly way to Peter.

"Come along! Be quick!" he said. "We must be off. But wrap up well, for it's cold outside."

"Where are we going to?" asked little Peter. "Into the cave? And is Mamma going too?"

"No," said the little man. "She's stopping at home. But do be quick, for the feast has begun."

And with that he gave such a jump on to the floor that the boards fairly creaked again, and little Peter, slipped out of bed after him. The little Parsnip-man helped him on with his shoes and stockings, and Peter put on the rest of his clothes himself.

Then the Mannikin pulled out a little whistle and blew on it. Immediately there was a rustling under the bed, and then two mice peeped out.

In a moment the Parsnip-man caught one, and vaulted on to its back.

"You get on the other," he said to Peter.

"But it isn't big enough to carry me," said Peter doubtfully.

"Get up, I tell you!" said the little man, laughing.

Peter did as he was told. Doubtless he had been growing smaller, for when he was fairly astride he sat the mouse as if it had been made for him. As to the mouse, it kept perfectly still for Peter to mount.

"Now, sit fast!" cried the Mannikin; and Peter had hardly seized the ears of the mouse (for want of reins), when his new steed ran away with him under the bed.

Then all of a sudden it became quite dark.

"Where are we?" cried Peter, for the mouse galloped on, and Peter was getting frightened.

"We are in the cellar," the voice of the Parsnip-man replied at his side. "Don't be frightened; it will be light again in a minute or two."

Accordingly, in a few moments, Peter could see all around him. They had emerged from the cellar, and were now in the street. The wind had fallen, and there was a dead calm. The street-lamps were burning with a somewhat dim light, however.

Peter could now plainly see the form of the little Parsnip-man riding beside him. The mice scampered on and on.

A watchman was standing in the doorway of a house. His halberd reposed against the wall beside him. Probably the watchman himself was reposing, for he never moved when the mice and their riders went by. They rode to the end of the street, and there, before an old deserted house which Peter had often shuddered to look at in the daytime, the mice stopped.

"Here we are!" said the Parsnip-man, jumping down from his mouse.

Peter dismounted more leisurely, and the two mice ran off.

It was almost pitch dark by the old house. Only one distant lamp gave a feeble glimmer. The Parsnip-man whistled as before. By and by Peter heard a sound like "Bst! bst!"

He looked all round, but could see nothing. At this moment the Mannikin caught him by the arm and pointed upwards to a hole in the wall of the old house. Peter then perceived that something was moving higher up, and very shortly he heard a rustling noise as if a ladder of ropes were being let down from above.

"Come quickly!" said a shrill, slender voice. "The chimes have sounded once since the hour. The Queen is waiting."

"Climb on to my shoulders, Peter," said the Parsnip-man, stooping as he spoke. Peter did so, and held fast by the little man's neck, who climbed nimbly up the rope-ladder to the opening in the wall above; and there Peter got down.

Here there stood another Parsnip-man with a little lantern in his hand, which he turned on Peter's face, and then nodded to him in a friendly way. After which he unhooked the rope-ladder and drew it up.

The two Parsnip-men now took Peter between them, each holding a hand. They went through long dark passages, and then they began to go down-stairs. Peter counted a hundred steps, but still they went down, down, and he could count no more.

All at once he heard music, which sounded as if it came from a distance. They were now at the bottom of the steps, and walking on level ground. The further they went the louder grew the music, and at last the Parsnip-men came to a standstill.

The one who held the lantern threw its light upon the wall till it disclosed a knob, on which he pressed. Then he put out his lantern, and all was dark. But the music sounded louder than before.

Suddenly the wall parted and moved aside, and Peter could hardly restrain his cries of astonishment, for what he now saw was like nothing he had ever seen before. He was looking into a great big hall. It was as light as day. Dazzling lustres of crystal, with thousands and thousands of wax tapers, whose flames were reflected from the mirrors suspended round the room, hung from the roof. Strange music shook the walls, and to the time of this music hundreds and hundreds of little Parsnip-men twirled and danced. All of them were dressed in yellow coats and green hats, and many of them wore long white beards. And oh, how they chirped and smirked, and laughed and jumped about, as if they were mad!

For a long time Peter stood bewildered. At last the little Parsnip-men who had brought him so far led him right into the room, and the wall closed behind them.

"Now for the Queen!" whispered one of them. "Come along."

They went down the side of the room, against the wall of which were ranged chairs with grand purple coverings and gilded arms. Once or twice Peter nearly slipped, so polished was the floor. From time to time some little Parsnip-man in the company nodded to him; otherwise no one paid much attention to him.

In this way they reached the farther end of the hall, where there was a throne, raised on a dais and covered by a canopy hung with purple. It was something like the throne Peter once saw when his aunt took him with her to the palace. A few steps led up to the throne, with a wonderfully elaborate balustrade made of gold.

The little mannikins seized his hands and led him up the steps between them. Then they drew back the purple curtains, and displayed a grand throne on which was seated a little girl in a snow-white dress. On her head she wore a little gold crown, from which hung a long transparent veil. She was resting her head on her hand, and did not look up till Peter and the Parsnip-men were quite close to her. Then she gave a cry of joy.

"So you've come at last, Peter!" she cried, her eyes brightening with delight; and as she took his hand, he saw that she was no other than his favourite playfellow and neighbour, little Mary.

There was a second seat beside her, and to this she drew Peter. Then she beckoned to the Parsnip-men, and said, "You have got everything ready, have you not?" The Parsnip-men bowed low, and hurried away.

In a minute or two they returned, followed by about thirty mannikins like themselves, who bore a magnificent dress which they deposited before Peter. There was a coat of blue silk, turned up with fur, and trimmed with precious stones. Besides this there were knee-breeches of the same material, slashed with white and fringed with gold, white silk stockings, and smart shoes with gold buckles. To complete the whole, there lay on the top a cap, with a heron's plume fastened by an aigrette of gold.

But Peter's attention all this time had been fixed upon Mary. He fancied she looked bigger than usual and unfamiliar in some way.

"Take the clothes into that room," said she to the little men; "and you, Peter," she added, "go with them and dress. Then we will go to supper."

"But—er—does your mamma know you're here?" asked Peter. He could not get over his amazement at the style and tone in which little Mary issued her orders in this strange place.

"I should think not!" laughed the little girl. "But never mind, Peter: we shall soon be at home again. What you've got to do just now is to put on your things."

As if in a dream, Peter went into the room into which the clothes had been taken, and where the little men helped him to take off his things and dress himself in his new-finery. Some of them then brought a long mirror, in which Peter could see himself from head to foot, and he fairly laughed with delight at his fine appearance in his new clothes.

Then the little men led him back to the Queen, who looked him well over, and she also smiled complacently.

"Did you bring your doll, Mary?" said Peter presently.

"That's not very likely," replied she. "It would not do for a queen to play at dolls."

"Have you been a queen very long?" Peter inquired.

"For several years," said Mary.

"But you and I were playing together only yesterday," said poor Peter, in puzzled tones.

But Mary had turned her back to him, and was pulling a bell at the back of her throne.

Although the music was still going on, the clear tone of the bell which the Queen had rung was heard above every other sound.

The music and the dancing stopped at once.

"Come, Peter, give me your arm," said Mary. "We're going into the supper-room."

They stepped down into the hall, where all the Parsnip-men had now ranged themselves in two long rows, down the centre of which the Queen and her companion now passed, and then the Parsnip-men closed in and formed a long procession behind them.

In this way they came to the other end of the hall. The large folding-doors swung open, and Peter fancied he was looking into a large garden. But it was only another hall in which tall foreign-looking trees were planted, whilst many-tinted flowers of gorgeous colours and strange shapes hung from the walls, and hither and thither among them flitted curious birds of many hues. As in the first hall, crystal lustres with wax tapers descended from the roof, and in the middle of the room, to which they now advanced, was a long table covered with a white table-cloth, and laid out with gold and silver plate of all sorts. There were golden vases with handles, golden tankards, golden dessert-dishes filled with splendid fruits; silver plates and goblets and drinking-cups, and beside them stood crystal flasks. Hundreds of chairs were placed round the table, and in every place was a little silver knife and a plate.

Peter could not gaze long enough. He wanted to stop every moment, but Mary only laughed, and dragged him on.

About the middle of the long table there was a dais raised above the level on which the other chairs and table stood. It was covered by a canopy of yellow silk, and under this was a table more richly laid out than the big one, and two seats of pure gold. To this Mary led Peter, and then said emphatically—"These are *our* seats."

Up they climbed, and then Mary dropped Peter's arm and sat down on one of the seats, and he seated himself beside her on the other.

From his present elevation Peter was well able to observe the Parsnip-men as they passed by in procession, and took their places on the chairs.

When all were seated the music recommenced. Then out of a side door came about fifty mannikins carrying large cakes on silver dishes, which they set down on the long table, and having cut them up handed them round to the guests. Others poured red or golden wine from the vases into the goblets. Everybody ate and drank, and chatted and laughed between-whiles.

Among the golden dishes on the golden table where Peter and Mary sat, was one which held a cake which had a particularly inviting smell. Mary cut a piece off and put it on to Peter's golden plate. Then, from a beautiful golden goblet, she poured ruby-coloured wine into their crystal glasses.

Peter ate and drank with great relish, and soon disposed of the cake and wine.

"I should like to have some of that beautiful fruit, too, if I may," said he. And as he spoke Mary filled his plate with grapes, apples, and pears.

"Eat away, Peter!" said she, laughing till her white teeth shone through her lips. "Don't be afraid of emptying the dish. There is plenty more fruit if we want it."

"I should like to take some home to Mamma," said Peter, biting into an apple. "May I, Mary?"

Mary nodded kindly, and handed him a golden dish full of sweetmeats, saying, "Put as many of these into your pocket as you like." And he filled his pockets accordingly.

Peter felt as happy as a king. His head was quite turned. He shouted aloud for joy, and swung his legs backwards and forwards as he sat on his golden chair.

"But I say, Mary," said he, laughing, "we shall go on playing together the same as ever, sha'n't we? I shall bring my leaden soldiers, and you'll bring your dolls again, won't you?"

But at this moment Mary seized his arm, and whispered in a frightened voice—"Hush, Peter, hush! Don't you hear?"

The music had suddenly ceased, and with it all the talking and laughing at the long table, and in the silence the sound of the church clock could be distinctly heard. *It struck one.*

At one stroke—the lights went out, a blast of wind blew through the banqueting-room, and then all was as still as death.

*   *   *   *   *

LEFT ALONE IN THE DARK—MOTHER—THE PARSNIP-MAN BY DAYLIGHT—THREE POUNDS.

    Juliana Horatia Ewing

Peter sat in his chair, as if petrified with terror, Mary still holding fast by his arm.

"Quick, quick!" she cried, breathlessly. "We must get away from here." Then she let his arm go, and hurried away from him.

"Wait, wait!" he cried, anxiously; "I don't know where I am. Take me with you, Mary! I can't see my way. Mary! Mary! Mary!"

Nobody replied.

Peter slid down from his chair and groped his way forward till he knocked against the corner of the table. Terror fairly overcame him, and he cried—"Mother! Mother! Mother!"

"What's the matter, dear?" said his mother's gentle voice.

"I am here, Mother," cried Peter; "but I am so frightened! Mary has run away and left me all alone in the dark hall."

"Come, Peter, come; collect yourself," said his mother, who was standing by the bed where poor Peter was sitting straight up with an anxious face, down which big tears were running.

"You're here, Peter, you know; in your own little bed," said his mother, putting her arms round him.

Peter began to take heart a little, and looked round him with big wide-open eyes.

"But how did I get here?" he asked, still stupefied with sleep.

"You've never been anywhere else, you know," said his mother.

"But I know the Parsnip-man took me away, and I rode on the mouse, too," said little Peter.

"Nonsense, nonsense; you're still dreaming. There, get up and put on your clothes."

"But I want the other clothes, the beautiful blue dress. These things are so dreadfully patched and darned," said Peter, in a lamentable tone. "And I have brought something nice for you too, Mother dear. It's in the pockets of the blue coat."

"You haven't got a blue coat, child," said his mother. "Come, come. Put on your clothes and come into the warm kitchen." And she carried Peter out into the arm-chair by the breakfast-table, and began to pour out some coffee for him. And she put the Parsnip-man (who had been lying all night behind the stove) into his hand. "See," she continued, "here's your Parsnip-man, about whom you have been dreaming all this fine nonsense."

Peter examined it with eager eyes. It looked exactly the same as it had done the night before.

"But Mary was there too," he said, still doubtfully. "She is the Queen of the Parsnip-men, you know. And she gave me cake and wine and fruit."

"Well, we'll ask her about it next time she comes," said his mother, laughing.

Just then there was a knock at the door. The mother hastened to open it, and found a messenger waiting with a letter in his hand which had several seals on it. It was addressed to herself, and beside the address was written, "*Three pounds enclosed*." Having given a small sum to the messenger for his trouble, the widow broke the seals of the letter with

Juliana Horatia Ewing

trembling fingers. The three pounds were duly enclosed, but no letter accompanied the welcome money.

Overcome with joy, the widow seized Peter, who had crept curiously to her side, in her arms and exclaimed with delight, "Ah! you shall have a nice blue dress, after all, my child."

But when the boy asked, "Who has sent us all this money, Mother?" all she could say was, "I wish I knew, my dear. But you see there is no letter with it."

Then Peter smiled expressively, but said nothing, for he thought—"Mother won't believe me, I know. But who can the money have come from, except from the little Parsnip-man?"

A CHILD'S WISHES

(From the German of R. Reinick.)

A certain old knight had a little daughter called Gertrude; and when his brother died, leaving an only son, he took the boy into his castle, and treated him as his own son. The boy's name was Walter. The two children lived together like brother and sister; they only played where they could play together, and were of one heart and of one soul. But one day, when Gertrude had gone out alone to pick flowers beyond the castle gate, some gipsies came along the high-road, who stole the child and took her away. No one knew what had become of her; the poor old father died of grief, and Walter wept long days and nights for his Gertrude.

At last there came a warm spring day, when the trees began to bud, and Walter went out into the wood. There, in a beautiful green spot, a brook bubbled under the trees, where he had often sat with Gertrude, floating little boats of nutshells on the stream. He sat down there now, cut himself a hazel stick for a hobby-horse, and as he did so he said to himself—

"Ah! if I were but a grown-up knight, as tall and stately as those who used to come to my uncle's castle, I would ride out into the wide world and look for Gertrude!"

218   Juliana Horatia Ewing

Meanwhile, he heard something screaming near him, and when he looked up he saw a raven, which was stuck so fast between two branches of a tree that it could not move, whilst a snake was gliding towards it to devour it. Walter hastily seized his stick, beat the snake to death, and set the raven free.

"A thousand thanks, my dear child!" said the raven, who had flown up into a tree, from which he spoke—"a thousand thanks! And now, since you have saved my life, wish for whatever you like, and it shall be granted immediately. A year hence we will speak of this again."

When Walter heard this, he saw at once that the raven was an enchanted bird, and exclaimed with joy—

"I should like to be a noble knight with a helmet and a shield, a charger and a sword!"

All happened just as he wished. In an instant he was a tall, stately knight; his shield stood near him, and his hobby-horse became a proud charger, which, to show that it was no ghost, but a real horse of flesh and blood, began then and there to drink out of the stream.

At first, Walter could not think what had happened to him, but stood as if he were in a dream. Soon, however, a new life seemed to wake within him; he swung himself on to his horse with all the energy of youth, and rode far out into the land to look for little Gertrude.

Like other knights, he met with many adventures on his way. There was always something to contend with, either wild beasts or else knights, who, like himself, roved about the country delighting to find any one with whom they could do battle. On every occasion, however, Walter came off conqueror, for he was far more valiant than any of his opponents.

At last, one day he came within sight of a mountain, on which stood a high castle belonging to a certain queen. As he reached the summit, he saw from afar a little maiden, who sat playing with her doll before the castle gate, and when he drew nearer he found that it was his little Gertrude. Then he put spurs to his horse and shouted joyfully—

"Good-day, dear Gertrude!" But the child knew him not. As he drew nearer, he called again: "It is I indeed!—it is Cousin Walter!" but the child believed him not. And when he sprang from his horse to kiss her, and his armour, sword, and spurs rattled and clashed as he did so, the child was afraid that this strange man would hurt her, and she ran away back into the castle.

Poor Walter was very much troubled. He went in, however, and presented himself to the queen, who received him very graciously. He told her all that had happened, and learnt from her that she had bought Gertrude from the gipsies. But when he begged that she would let him take his dear little cousin away with him, she consented only on condition that the child herself should be willing, for Gertrude had become very dear to the old queen. So she called the little maid in, and said—

"Now look here, my child: this really is your Cousin Walter. Do you no longer love him, and will you not go away with him?"

The child looked at the knight from head to foot, and then said in a troubled voice—

"Since you both declare that it is Walter, I suppose I must

believe it. Ah! if only he were still as little as he was a year ago, I would go into the wide world with him, wherever he wanted; but now, I never can. It would be no good, whilst he is like that. If I wanted to play hide-and-seek, as we used to do, his armour would shine, and his spurs rattle, and I should know where he was directly. If I wanted to go to school with him, he could not sit by me on the little benches at the little tables. Then what could a poor child like me do for such a stately knight? If I tried to work for him, I should burn my little hands; if I tried to make his clothes, I should prick my little fingers; and if I ran races with him, I should hurt my little feet. If I were a grown-up princess, indeed, it would be a different thing."

Walter could not but feel that what Gertrude said was true. So he took leave of them both, mounted his horse, and rode away; but the queen and Gertrude watched him from the battlements of the castle.

He had not ridden many steps when a voice from a tree called "Walter! Walter!" and when he looked up, there was the raven, who said—

"A year has passed since you wished to be a knight. If you have another wish, speak, and it shall be granted; but observe, what you wished before will then be at an end."

To these last words Walter paid no attention. The raven had no sooner said that he might have another wish than he interrupted it, exclaiming: "Then I wish Gertrude to be a grown-up princess!"

But even as he spoke he himself became a child again, and his horse a hobby-horse, just as they had been a year ago. But when he looked up to the battlements, there stood by the queen a wonderfully beautiful princess, tall and slim and stately; and this was—his Gertrude! Then the boy, taking his hobby-horse, went back up to the castle steps, and wept bitterly. But the queen was sorry for him, took him in, and tried to comfort him.

And now there was another trouble. Dearly as the Princess Gertrude and the boy Walter loved each other, they were not so happy as they should have been. If Walter said to her, "Come, Gertrude, and we'll run races, and jump over the ditches," she would answer, "Oh! that would never do for a princess; what would people say?"

If Walter said, "Come and play hide-and-seek," Gertrude would answer again, "Oh! but that would never do for a princess; I should leave my train hanging on the thorns, and my coronet would be tumbling off my head."

Then if Gertrude asked Walter to bring in some venison for the table, the boy would bring her a mouse instead; and if a bull or a mad dog came after them, Gertrude must snatch Walter up in her arms, and run off with him, for she was so much bigger than he, and could run a great deal quicker. Meanwhile he remained in the castle, and the boy became very dear to the old queen.

Another year passed by, and one morning Gertrude sat under a tree in the garden with her embroidery, whilst Walter played at her feet. Then, as before, a voice called out of the tree, "Walter! Walter!" And when the boy looked up, the raven was sitting on a branch, who said: "Now once more you may wish, and it shall be granted; but this is the last time, therefore think it well over."

But Walter did not think long before he answered: "Ah! let us both be children all our lives long."

And as he wished so it happened. They both became children as before, played together more happily than ever, and were of one heart and of one soul.

But when another year had passed by, and the children sat plucking flowers and singing together in the garden, an angel flew down from heaven, who took them both in his arms and carried them away—away to the celestial gardens of Paradise, where they are yet together, gathering the flowers that never fade, and singing songs so wondrously beautiful, that even the blessed angels hear with joy.

WAR AND THE DEAD

A DRAMATIC DIALOGUE

(*From the French of Jean Mace.*)

Dramatis Personae.

Peace.
War.
A French Grenadier.
A German Hussar.
A Scotch Highlander.
A Cossack.
A Russian Peasant Woman.
A French Peasant Woman.
A German Peasant Woman.
An English Peasant Woman.

Soldiers *are lying on the ground.* Peace *is seated at the back, leaning her elbow on one knee, her head resting on her hand.*

Enter War.

War. To-day is the 18th of June, the anniversary of the battle of Waterloo, the day of a wrath which still mutters, and of a hatred yet unappeased. Let us employ it in re-animating this torpid century, which succumbs to the coward sweetness of an inglorious peace. After forty years of forced repose brighter days seemed at last to have returned to me. Twice did I unfurl the old colours in the breeze; twice I made hearts beat as of old at the magic din of battles; and twice that hateful Peace, rising suddenly before me, snatched the yet rusty sword from my hands.

Up! up! O heroes of great battles! you whom twenty-five years of warfare did not satiate: rise from your graves and shame your degenerate successors. Up! up! Bid some remember that they have a revenge to take, and tell others that they are not yet enough avenged.

Peace *rises*.

Peace. What do you want here, relentless War? Dispute the world of the living with me if you will, but at least respect the peace of the grave.

War. I have a right to summon the Dead when it is in the name of their country.

Peace. The Dead are with God; they have but one country among them.

War. You may dispense with set speeches, most eloquent Peace, for I pay no attention to them. I go forward, and leave talk to chatterers. The world belongs to the brave.

Peace. The world belongs to those who are in the right. Since, however, you will not listen to me, you shall hear the Dead themselves, and see if they agree with you. (*Turns to the* Dead.) Arise, my children; come and confound those who wish to fight with the bones of the departed.

The Dead *rise.*

Grenadier. I have slept a long time since Austerlitz. Who are you, comrades?

Hussar. I come from the battle-field of Leipsic, where the great German race broke the yoke which your Emperor had laid upon it.

Grenadier. You were left upon the field?

Hussar. I am proud to say so.

Grenadier. And you are right, old fellow; every man owes himself to his country. We others have done just the same. If you had let us alone in '92 we should not have come to you.

Cossack. I was killed under the walls of Paris, where great Russia went to return the insult she had received at Moscow.

Highlander. I fell at Waterloo, avenging the great English people for the threats of the camp at Boulogne. I drowned in my blood the last effort of your Imperial Eagle.

Grenadier. Well! we are well matched. My blood reddened the plain of Austerlitz, where the great French nation was avenged on Brunswick and Souwaroff. We have all perished, buried in a triumph. We can shake hands upon it.

Cossack. Brave men are equals, in whatever dress. Let us shake hands.

Hussar. We have all died for our country. Let us be brothers.

Highlander. Let us be brothers. The hatreds of earth do not extend beyond the grave.

[They join hands.]

Grenadier. And now Peace is proclaimed, let us tell each other what we used to do before we became warriors.

Cossack. I cultivated a piece of ground in the steppes and took care of my old mother.

Highlander. I brought up my daughter by farming a piece of ground which I had cleared on my native heath.

Hussar. I lived with my wife on the piece of land which we cultivated.

Grenadier. I tilled a piece of ground also, and supported my sister. It seems that we were all four of the same way of life. How did we come to kill one another?

Cossack. The Czar spoke, and I marched.

Highlander. Parliament voted for war, and I marched.

Hussar. Our princes cried, "To arms!" and I marched.

Grenadier. As for me, my comrades cried, "To arms!" and I put on my best sabots. But after all, what have we against each other? Where was the quarrel between our respective ploughshares? (*To the* Hussar.) You, for instance, who began, what did you come into my country for?

Hussar. We came to destroy brigands.

Grenadier. Brigands! That is to say, my unfortunate self, and other labourers like you and me. After this, well might we be made to sing about

"Vile blood soaking our furrows!"

I see now this "vile blood" was yours, my friend, and that of brave men like you. Cursed be those who forced us to fight together!

Hussar. Cursed be the contrivers of War!

War (*advancing*). Shame on you, degraded warriors! Your very wives would disown you. (*The* Dead *gaze fixedly.*) You are silent! What have you to answer?

Peace. The Dead do not reply. (*Points with her hand to the stage entrance.*) These shall answer for them.

Enter Four Veiled Women.

[*One of the* Veiled Women *slowly advances. When in front of the stage she lifts her veil, and is seen by the audience. The others afterwards do the same.*]

First Woman. Oh, my brother! where are you now? If you are ill, who nurses you? If you are wounded, who watches over you? If you are a prisoner, who comforts you? If you are dead—Alas! every night I go to rest weeping, because I have had no news of you; and every morning I awake dreading to receive it. We were so happy! We lived so comfortably together! and now I sit at our little table, with your empty place before me, and cannot eat for looking at it. Yet I made you promise to come back when we said good-bye. Ah! unkind! Why are you so long in fulfilling your promise?

[*She closes her veil and crosses to one side of the stage. The others afterwards do the same.*]

Grenadier. It is my sister, friends. She is repeating the words of our last adieu.

Second Woman. Oh, my father! why have you left your child? Alas! when you went away I played—poor fool!—with your brilliant uniform. (Dark livery of death, would that I had never seen thee!) I said I should be proud of you when you came back to me, having killed a great many of your enemies. Child that I was to speak of killing, not knowing what it meant! And now, when will you return? What have they done with you, dear Father? What has become of that revered head, which my lips never approached but with respect? Perhaps at this very moment it is dragged, all stained and livid, through the dust or in the mud. Oh, God! if my prayers may still avail for him, withdraw him speedily from those frightful conflicts, where every blow falls upon a father, a son, a brother, or a husband. Pity the many tears that flow for every drop of blood!

Highlander. It is my daughter! I yet hear the last farewell her innocent mouth sent after me.

Third Woman. Oh, my beloved! where can I go to look for you? Little did we think, when we vowed before God never in this life to forsake each other, that War would come and carry you away as a leaf is driven before the wind. Perhaps at this moment you are stretched upon an armful of bloody straw, and other hands than mine dress your glorious wounds. Ah, miserable me! of what does my tender jealousy complain? Who knows if you are not by this time safe from wounds for ever? Oh, my God! if Thou hast taken him, take me also. I promised to follow him when I received his parting kiss.

Hussar. It is my wife beyond a doubt! I recognize the words her sweet voice murmured that very day in my ear.

Fourth Woman. I said, "Go, and bear yourself like a man." He went, and he has not returned. Ah, merciless tigers! we rear our children with fear and weeping. We pass whole nights bent over their little cradles, and when we have made men of them you come and take them away from us that you may send them to death. And we, miserable women! must encourage them to die if we would not have them dishonoured. Poor dear boy! so strong! so handsome! so good to his mother! Ah! if there be a God of vengeance, surely the cries of desolate mothers will allow no sleep to those who provoke such massacres. They will haunt them to the grave, and rise behind them to the foot of that throne where the great Judge of all awaits them.

[*She buries her face in her hands.*]

Cossack. It is my mother! I recognize her last words. (*He springs towards her.*) It is I, Mother, it is I! (*She raises her head.*) What do I see? A stranger! and it is an Englishwoman!

Highlander (*raising the daughter's veil*). Good heavens! She is a German.

Hussar (*raising the wife's veil*). It is not she! It is a Frenchwoman.

Grenadier (*raising the sister's veil*). She is a Russian! It is not for us that they are weeping; perhaps it is for some of those whom we have killed. How could we be so deceived?

Peace (*advancing*). There are sisters, wives, daughters, and mothers everywhere, my children, and Nature has but one language in all countries. (*To WAR.*) As for you, go and sound your trumpet in barracks and drinking-houses, but invoke the Dead no more, and do not reckon upon women.

Choose from Thousands of 1stWorldLibrary Classics By

A. M. Barnard
Ada Leverson
Adolphus William Ward
Aesop
Agatha Christie
Alexander Aaronsohn
Alexander Kielland
Alexandre Dumas
Alfred Gatty
Alfred Ollivant
Alice Duer Miller
Alice Turner Curtis
Alice Dunbar
Allen Chapman
Alleyne Ireland
Ambrose Bierce
Amelia E. Barr
Amory H. Bradford
Andrew Lang
Andrew McFarland Davis
Andy Adams
Angela Brazil
Anna Alice Chapin
Anna Sewell
Annie Besant
Annie Hamilton Donnell
Annie Payson Call
Annie Roe Carr
Annonaymous
Anton Chekhov
Archibald Lee Fletcher
Arnold Bennett
Arthur C. Benson
Arthur Conan Doyle
Arthur M. Winfield
Arthur Ransome
Arthur Schnitzler
Arthur Train
Atticus
B.H. Baden-Powell
B. M. Bower
B. C. Chatterjee
Baroness Emmuska Orczy
Baroness Orczy
Basil King
Bayard Taylor
Ben Macomber
Bertha Muzzy Bower
Bjornstjerne Bjornson

Booth Tarkington
Boyd Cable
Bram Stoker
C. Collodi
C. E. Orr
C. M. Ingleby
Carolyn Wells
Catherine Parr Traill
Charles A. Eastman
Charles Amory Beach
Charles Dickens
Charles Dudley Warner
Charles Farrar Browne
Charles Ives
Charles Kingsley
Charles Klein
Charles Hanson Towne
Charles Lathrop Pack
Charles Romyn Dake
Charles Whibley
Charles Willing Beale
Charlotte M. Braeme
Charlotte M. Yonge
Charlotte Perkins Stetson
Clair W. Hayes
Clarence Day Jr.
Clarence E. Mulford
Clemence Housman
Confucius
Coningsby Dawson
Cornelis DeWitt Wilcox
Cyril Burleigh
D. H. Lawrence
Daniel Defoe
David Garnett
Dinah Craik
Don Carlos Janes
Donald Keyhoe
Dorothy Kilner
Dougan Clark
Douglas Fairbanks
E. Nesbit
E. P. Roe
E. Phillips Oppenheim
E. S. Brooks
Earl Barnes
Edgar Rice Burroughs
Edith Van Dyne
Edith Wharton

Edward Everett Hale
Edward J. O'Biren
Edward S. Ellis
Edwin L. Arnold
Eleanor Atkins
Eleanor Hallowell Abbott
Eliot Gregory
Elizabeth Gaskell
Elizabeth McCracken
Elizabeth Von Arnim
Ellem Key
Emerson Hough
Emilie F. Carlen
Emily Bronte
Emily Dickinson
Enid Bagnold
Enilor Macartney Lane
Erasmus W. Jones
Ernie Howard Pie
Ethel May Dell
Ethel Turner
Ethel Watts Mumford
Eugene Sue
Eugenie Foa
Eugene Wood
Eustace Hale Ball
Evelyn Everett-green
Everard Cotes
F. H. Cheley
F. J. Cross
F. Marion Crawford
Fannie E. Newberry
Federick Austin Ogg
Ferdinand Ossendowski
Fergus Hume
Florence A. Kilpatrick
Fremont B. Deering
Francis Bacon
Francis Darwin
Frances Hodgson Burnett
Frances Parkinson Keyes
Frank Gee Patchin
Frank Harris
Frank Jewett Mather
Frank L. Packard
Frank V. Webster
Frederic Stewart Isham
Frederick Trevor Hill
Frederick Winslow Taylor

Friedrich Kerst
Friedrich Nietzsche
Fyodor Dostoyevsky
G.A. Henty
G.K. Chesterton
Gabrielle E. Jackson
Garrett P. Serviss
Gaston Leroux
George A. Warren
George Ade
Geroge Bernard Shaw
George Cary Eggleston
George Durston
George Ebers
George Eliot
George Gissing
George MacDonald
George Meredith
George Orwell
George Sylvester Viereck
George Tucker
George W. Cable
George Wharton James
Gertrude Atherton
Gordon Casserly
Grace E. King
Grace Gallatin
Grace Greenwood
Grant Allen
Guillermo A. Sherwell
Gulielma Zollinger
Gustav Flaubert
H. A. Cody
H. B. Irving
H.C. Bailey
H. G. Wells
H. H. Munro
H. Irving Hancock
H. R. Naylor
H. Rider Haggard
H. W. C. Davis
Haldeman Julius
Hall Caine
Hamilton Wright Mabie
Hans Christian Andersen
Harold Avery
Harold McGrath
Harriet Beecher Stowe
Harry Castlemon
Harry Coghill
Harry Houidini

Hayden Carruth
Helent Hunt Jackson
Helen Nicolay
Hendrik Conscience
Hendy David Thoreau
Henri Barbusse
Henrik Ibsen
Henry Adams
Henry Ford
Henry Frost
Henry James
Henry Jones Ford
Henry Seton Merriman
Henry W Longfellow
Herbert A. Giles
Herbert Carter
Herbert N. Casson
Herman Hesse
Hildegard G. Frey
Homer
Honore De Balzac
Horace B. Day
Horace Walpole
Horatio Alger Jr.
Howard Pyle
Howard R. Garis
Hugh Lofting
Hugh Walpole
Humphry Ward
Ian Maclaren
Inez Haynes Gillmore
Irving Bacheller
Isabel Cecilia Williams
Isabel Hornibrook
Israel Abrahams
Ivan Turgenev
J.G.Austin
J. Henri Fabre
J. M. Barrie
J. M. Walsh
J. Macdonald Oxley
J. R. Miller
J. S. Fletcher
J. S. Knowles
J. Storer Clouston
J. W. Duffield
Jack London
Jacob Abbott
James Allen
James Andrews
James Baldwin

James Branch Cabell
James DeMille
James Joyce
James Lane Allen
James Lane Allen
James Oliver Curwood
James Oppenheim
James Otis
James R. Driscoll
Jane Abbott
Jane Austen
Jane L. Stewart
Janet Aldridge
Jens Peter Jacobsen
Jerome K. Jerome
Jessie Graham Flower
John Buchan
John Burroughs
John Cournos
John F. Kennedy
John Gay
John Glasworthy
John Habberton
John Joy Bell
John Kendrick Bangs
John Milton
John Philip Sousa
John Taintor Foote
Jonas Lauritz Idemil Lie
Jonathan Swift
Joseph A. Altsheler
Joseph Carey
Joseph Conrad
Joseph E. Badger Jr
Joseph Hergesheimer
Joseph Jacobs
Jules Vernes
Julian Hawthrone
Julie A Lippmann
Justin Huntly McCarthy
Kakuzo Okakura
Karle Wilson Baker
Kate Chopin
Kenneth Grahame
Kenneth McGaffey
Kate Langley Bosher
Kate Langley Bosher
Katherine Cecil Thurston
Katherine Stokes
L. A. Abbot
L. T. Meade

L. Frank Baum
Latta Griswold
Laura Dent Crane
Laura Lee Hope
Laurence Housman
Lawrence Beasley
Leo Tolstoy
Leonid Andreyev
Lewis Carroll
Lewis Sperry Chafer
Lilian Bell
Lloyd Osbourne
Louis Hughes
Louis Joseph Vance
Louis Tracy
Louisa May Alcott
Lucy Fitch Perkins
Lucy Maud Montgomery
Luther Benson
Lydia Miller Middleton
Lyndon Orr
M. Corvus
M. H. Adams
Margaret E. Sangster
Margret Howth
Margaret Vandercook
Margaret W. Hungerford
Margret Penrose
Maria Edgeworth
Maria Thompson Daviess
Mariano Azuela
Marion Polk Angellotti
Mark Overton
Mark Twain
Mary Austin
Mary Catherine Crowley
Mary Cole
Mary Hastings Bradley
Mary Roberts Rinehart
Mary Rowlandson
M. Wollstonecraft Shelley
Maud Lindsay
Max Beerbohm
Myra Kelly
Nathaniel Hawthrone
Nicolo Machiavelli
O. F. Walton
Oscar Wilde

Owen Johnson
P.G. Wodehouse
Paul and Mabel Thorne
Paul G. Tomlinson
Paul Severing
Percy Brebner
Percy Keese Fitzhugh
Peter B. Kyne
Plato
Quincy Allen
R. Derby Holmes
R. L. Stevenson
R. S. Ball
Rabindranath Tagore
Rahul Alvares
Ralph Bonehill
Ralph Henry Barbour
Ralph Victor
Ralph Waldo Emmerson
Rene Descartes
Ray Cummings
Rex Beach
Rex E. Beach
Richard Harding Davis
Richard Jefferies
Richard Le Gallienne
Robert Barr
Robert Frost
Robert Gordon Anderson
Robert L. Drake
Robert Lansing
Robert Lynd
Robert Michael Ballantyne
Robert W. Chambers
Rosa Nouchette Carey
Rudyard Kipling
Saint Augustine
Samuel B. Allison
Samuel Hopkins Adams
Sarah Bernhardt
Sarah C. Hallowell
Selma Lagerlof
Sherwood Anderson
Sigmund Freud
Standish O'Grady
Stanley Weyman
Stella Benson
Stella M. Francis

Stephen Crane
Stewart Edward White
Stijn Streuvels
Swami Abhedananda
Swami Parmananda
T. S. Ackland
T. S. Arthur
The Princess Der Ling
Thomas A. Janvier
Thomas A Kempis
Thomas Anderton
Thomas Bailey Aldrich
Thomas Bulfinch
Thomas De Quincey
Thomas Dixon
Thomas H. Huxley
Thomas Hardy
Thomas More
Thornton W. Burgess
U. S. Grant
Upton Sinclair
Valentine Williams
Various Authors
Vaughan Kester
Victor Appleton
Victor G. Durham
Victoria Cross
Virginia Woolf
Wadsworth Camp
Walter Camp
Walter Scott
Washington Irving
Wilbur Lawton
Wilkie Collins
Willa Cather
Willard F. Baker
William Dean Howells
William le Queux
W. Makepeace Thackeray
William W. Walter
William Shakespeare
Winston Churchill
Yei Theodora Ozaki
Yogi Ramacharaka
Young E. Allison
Zane Grey